JAFFNA BOY

BERNARD SINNIAH

Copyright © 2014 Bernard Sinniah
All rights reserved.

ISBN: 1502743582
ISBN 13: 9781502743589

*This book is dedicated to all those
who tolerated me and
supported me over the years.*

Believe…believe…believe.
　　　—Achchi, in the train

PREFACE

"Ha-ha…We had great fun. Anita, have you heard this story before?"

"Of course I have. That is all you talk about when you and Johnians meet."

My very good friend Mohan Thavaratnam was visiting us from Canada in 2001. Every time we met, we just talked about our school days, recalling the wonderful times.

I decided that I must write all these stories and started this project, *Jaffna Boy*. It has taken me thirteen years to complete. As my dear Mahendran master once said, "Nothing is easy."

I am indebted to numerous people who helped me in writing this book. I am not able to recall all the names. Thank you for your support, guidance, and encouragement. I am very grateful to all.

Thank you for my family for putting up with me—then and now. Without them, I couldn't have completed this goal.

Enjoy *Jaffna Boy*!
Bernard Sinniah
Walton-on-Thames
2014

CONTENTS

Preface vii

1. The Mail Train 1
2. My Initial Years 10
3. The Memorial Block 56
4. The Rise and Fall of Somasundaram Avenue 100
5. The Return 122
6. The Advanced Levels 144
7. The Real Surprise of July '79 173
8. Thirty-Five Years On 179

About the Author 189

THE MAIL TRAIN

"FIVE MINUTES TO GO," BARKED THE HEAD EXAMINER.

"Why is this man shouting when there is a huge clock above his head? He seems to enjoy the power."

Applied Mathematics was the final paper of my advanced-level examination. This was my favourite subject. I stopped writing, glanced over my answer sheet, and made sure that I had written my name in the correct place. I numbered all the pages and inserted all the needed information. I had already finished answering, but I didn't have the courage to walk out of the exam hall. Normally, only those who hadn't done well would leave the exam hall way before the scheduled close. I didn't want to give that impression, especially since this was my last exam.

All throughout my school days, I had hated studying! But one has to do it to pass the year-end exams and move up to the next class. This examination was my last as a schoolboy, and I was determined to make a good impression to my fellow students. I had about forty minutes left on the clock. I read over my answer sheet ten times.

I knew what would happen. I had only about a 50 percent chance of passing, but I had given it my best. I always picked four or five topics and studied them very well. There were always eight questions, and you had to answer only five. I continually took this gamble; it mostly paid off and was always just enough for me to pass.

This time was another gamble. I was very lucky, as all the topics I had studied appeared on the question paper. I was very pleased. I gave a confident look to my fellow students. Here was a great opportunity to really do well in one subject. Not all in my class liked Applied Mathematics, but that didn't mean I could get more marks than them. This was it. The other three subjects were very difficult, and the maximum I could achieve would be a pass.

Now, with only five minutes to go, I was sweating profusely. I was panicking, not because of my potential results but because I knew that this was my last five minutes as a schoolboy. I had no clue what I would be doing after I left school. I would be going to Colombo, where my parents were living, and would have to take it from there.

As a student from this prestigious school, St. John's College, Jaffna, I was, simply put, a massive failure. I was not going to be a doctor or an engineer, or even enter the university with my A-level results. It was all too much for the five minutes, and my thought was to get out of the hall quickly. I walked out as if I had done very well. I gave the impression that I was sure to get an A, but I knew what my classmates thought of me. They knew that I was not a great student. Still, it was an amazing feeling. I didn't have to study anymore.

After the exam, I spoke to a few of my classmates, gave them my address in Colombo, and returned to Fleming Hostel. I had already packed my suitcases. I had my clothes and a few books in my Ford suitcase. I had very few clothes, though; I always borrowed from others. I packed a lot of sentimental stuff like old movie ticket stubs, old hymn sheets from the college carol services, posters of film stars, and old Tamil movie songbooks. I dumped all into a cardboard box. I had a very small suitcase that I dumped into the box, too, as with everything else around my bed. The box was very heavy.

It was time for good-byes. I had about an hour to go before leaving the college to go to Jaffna Railway Station. I thought I would say good-bye to my principal, Mr. C. E. Anandarajan. I liked him a lot. He was a great man. I had the privilege of being punished by him on numerous occasions, but I still liked him. He was so helpful to all of us and was a very generous man. He wished me well and told me to stay in touch with him. I was sure that he was worried about me. I knew exactly what he thought. He also thought what everyone else thought: *What will this guy do?*

I went to see my favourite teacher, Panchalingham master. His son, Shanthakumar, was my classmate; we had studied together for a long time. Mr. Panchalingham was in charge of the catering of the hostel and was also the vice principal of the college, a very well-respected man. He taught physics, and I had been his student, but definitely not the best.

I returned to Fleming to catch up with my hostel mates. This was very sad. I had been a hostel boy for ten years from the age of eight and a half, and this had been my home—perhaps my first. I loved it. I enjoyed every minute of it. Now, I had thirty minutes to get out of the way. I kept my emotions to myself, cracked a few jokes with my friends, and was ready to go.

One by one, everyone was going home. I was getting very emotional. It was now my turn. My two closest friends, Tharmakumar (Tharmu) and Joshua, who was my first cousin, were to take me to the railway station. Tharmu had an examination the next day, while Joshua lived in Jaffna. They were both there with their bicycles. I had no idea where Tharmu got his bicycle from, but Joshua had a lovely green Raleigh. I had learnt to ride on that bicycle. It was fitting that I left Jaffna on it. It brought back many good memories.

I got on the pillion of Joshua's green bicycle while Tharmu had my suitcase strapped to his. I held that heavy box in my hand as though it contained a lot of valuable things. I had packed it nicely on the outside. I didn't put a ribbon on it, but I wrapped some really nice brown paper on the outside and used a white rope to tie it up. This was impressive—the brown paper and the white rope. No one used white rope. Normally, all the ropes were brown. Mine looked like a very expensive rope. This was the rope that I got when I joined the Boy Scout movement. It had been my great-uncle's. I think he was dead by then.

We left Fleming and passed the dining room. All the cooks and their assistants were outside having a chat and saying goodbye to the students. This was a routine that always happened in front of the college dining room. They must have been relieved that we were going home. The A levels were normally held during the April holidays, and the cooks had to work during that period. It really annoyed them, because they didn't get any time off. They were lovely people.

Chelliah, the head cook, was standing outside with his cigar, a *chooruttu*. Ramu and Nagamuttu had been there since I joined. Ramu rarely wore a shirt, and I used to annoy him a lot by tickling him. Periayasamy and Kandasamy were brothers, and they had joined the school a few years ago. They were young and always joked around with us. Nagamuttu was a very serious man and took his duties seriously. He wore very thick glasses. He was strict and quiet. We rarely joked with him. The cooks were always very nice to me, but I had no doubt they must have been happy to see me leave. They told me to be a good boy and to behave well. Did that mean that I had been a naughty boy? I was very naughty, but I had great fun.

I passed the Jubilee hall where the examinations were held. There were still some students standing outside the hall, discussing the paper. These were the intellectuals and were sure to get an A for Applied Maths. I glanced at them to let them know that, if not for the train, I, too, would be standing with them.

We were now nearing the college gate. As boarders, we were never allowed to go out of the school premises unless we got special permission. I had spent a lot of time standing close to this gate, asking passers-by to buy me things from the shops near it. Sivaguru, our ice cream man, always stood there, too, but he was not there that day. He didn't cover our school during the holidays. By now, I felt really terrible and was crying. I couldn't believe that I was leaving. I didn't know what was in store for me. At eighteen, you couldn't cry openly. I cried inside me for a very long time.

At the gate, I met Mani and Benedict. Mani was our groundsman. He always wore a white shirt and a pair of white shorts. How could he be so clean and keep his clothes so white when he was a groundsman? Benedict was the gatekeeper. He was the son of the previous gatekeeper, who was also called Benedict. I was sure the next gatekeeper would be *his* son and be called

Benedict, too. They told me to remember them when I got a good job in Colombo. How they could think that amused me, I don't know, but I was very pleased that I had some admirers. I needed some comfort, and it was great to meet them as I was leaving St. John's College.

Tharmu and Joshua were expert cyclists and had no brakes on their bicycles. That was very common; we used our feet. We went out of the school and had a quick stop at Cheryl's. This was a joint we would go to for a cup of plain tea and an *adai*, which is a small pancake. It was reasonably hard to eat, but given what we paid, it was good enough. We used to go to Cheryl's often, as our school canteen didn't have much of a variety.

We then passed Tulips, another small boutique where we used to go for *koththu roti*, cheap but lovely food. We didn't stop there, as it was very spicy, and I had a very sensitive stomach. If I had eaten *koththu roti* then, I would have spent half of my train journey in the toilet.

We now turned into Temple Road. This was where a lot of young schoolboys met their girlfriends. There were a lot of houses that held tuition classes down this road. It was easy to go there to meet a girl, as the elders would think you were there to attend the classes. That was for others, not for me! Sadly, I didn't have a girlfriend to say good-bye to. I was determined that I would return one day to capture the heart of one of these girls.

Finally, we turned into Station Road, the last lap of my journey to the station. Every road that led to a railway station was called Station Road. You could bet that there would be a Main Street, a Station Road, a Temple Road, a Church Street, and a School Lane in every suburb of Jaffna.

I remembered the Toddy Tavern at the corner. Toddy was a great drink, but you could suffer afterwards. We had a lot of good drinking sessions there, but I'd only started visiting the tavern the previous year. This was to show that I had matured and that I could match the big boys. I was a terrible drinker. I went there for show, to prove a point, but ended up always getting sick.

Then we were at Jaffna Station. I had prebooked tickets. My father had bought me sleeperette tickets, so they were reserved. The mail train left Kankensanthurai around six in the evening and arrived in Colombo at six the next morning. It was a long, twelve-hour journey for two hundred and forty miles. It stopped at all stations, collected and delivered mail, and moved very slowly. That is why it was called the mail train. It was now due to arrive in Jaffna in fifteen minutes' time.

I had fifteen minutes to go—fifteen valuable minutes. I would never forget those fifteen minutes, even though they passed very quickly. There were a lot of people on that platform. There were friends of mine who had come to say good-bye to me. I made sure that I spoke to all of them, and then I saw the mail train approaching. I had a look at my closest friends—Tharmu and Joshua—and all I did was hug both of them. I got into the train as quickly as I could. I knew I was crying, but again, being a big boy, I didn't show that to anyone.

I found my seat, which was next to a very old lady. I always had a dream of travelling on a train and sitting next to a very good-looking young girl. It never happened to me—always an old lady or an old man. Today was no surprise!

"Achchi, I will just get down for a few minutes and come back." We always called old ladies "Achchi." It made them feel we had a lot of respect. This pleased her.

I now got down from the compartment to say my final goodbyes. It is a customary boy thing to get off the train and only jump back on when the guard blows his whistle. I had to do it, and this time it was special. I jumped on after shaking hands with everyone and waited until the train started to move. I wanted to show off to my friends that I was not only a big boy but had some style too! I was sure they would remember me for the way I jumped onto the train, as there was nothing much else to remember me for. I didn't light up the school with extraordinary performances in anything—studies or sports.

I had a seat next to the window. I had my head out and waved to my friends. I waved as long as I could see them. It was a long wave, but I was a bit scared, as I didn't want to hit my head against those railway posts. Achchi was very impressed but asked me to get my head in. There was no point in impressing her. She was a great-grandmother. I closed the window and sat down.

I had no clue where this train would take me in my life. I knew I was entering some unknown world, and I was very scared.

The next eleven hours were difficult. I was very lost. What would I be doing next? Where would I end up? I was a failure by Jaffna standards. A good Jaffna boy had to study hard, enter university, and become a doctor or an engineer. After that, get married around his midtwenties and have two kids. I had no chance. It was amazing how success was defined. I definitely didn't fit into any of those high standards, and I didn't know what I wanted to do or even what I was capable of.

It was time to reflect, but I thought I would go to sleep. I was very good at that. I could sleep anywhere, anytime, and in any position. It was a rare talent, though no one gave me any credit or even talked about it to the girls. I was an expert sleeper. I fell asleep whenever I opened my books to study, and that was why I was hopeless at studies. I liked storybooks, but again, after reading two or three pages, I could easily fall into a nice sleep.

I was leaving Jaffna and St. John's College for good. I was leaving as a failed Jaffna boy. We were nearing Navatkuli when Achchi woke me up. She offered me *kachchan* (peanuts). It had been five minutes since we had left Jaffna, and I was already asleep. This *kachchan* offer really irritated me. I took some and tried to sleep. It was a different sleep this time, and my dreams took me back to that day.

MY INITIAL YEARS

THAT DAY WAS THE FIRST SUNDAY IN MAY 1968. I remember that day very well. It was the beginning of my stay at St. John's College, Jaffna. My father drove me to the school with my mother and my two older brothers. We always called my parents Dadda and Mummy. To show respect to our older brothers, I called them Anna: Ranjit Anna and Wijit Anna were my older brothers. I was eight and a half years old. I was very nervous.

Dadda's Morris Minor 1000, 2 Sri 6989, pulled up at the college gate and parked outside the office block. I saw Dadda going into the office, paying the fees, and doing some paperwork. He then spoke to one of the teachers and his good friend, Mr. H. W. Canagarajah. They talked for some time and laughed a lot. I thought that it might be something about me.

We went over to drop my brothers at their boarding houses. Ranjit Anna went to Handy Hostel while Wijit Anna went to Thompson Hostel. They got down, kissed my parents good-bye, and went straight into their hostels. They both had a trunk for clothes and a suitcase for books. My father gave them twenty rupees each. This looked good. You got cash for going to school. I waited for my turn.

We went past a few buildings, past the college grounds where some students were playing cricket, and went to a corner of the school. I saw a long building, and a few cars were parked outside. A small boy, shorter and younger than me, was clenching his mother's hands and crying very loudly. I didn't know that he was joining the hostel. I thought he was a younger brother of one of the boarders.

My parents and I then went inside this long building. It had no rooms and was like a warehouse. It had about forty beds. There was an older boy there, directing everyone. My father gave a piece of paper to him, and he smiled and welcomed us in. He was the college prefect and was in charge of our hostel. His name was Mahadevan. He looked much older, but he was only eighteen.

I had two suitcases; the smaller one was to take my books to school every day while the larger contained all my clothes. I also had a small quilt. The beds were made of two flat pieces of wood joined together and four legs. I was allocated a bed next to Wijeyanathan and Maheswaran, who was the small boy I had seen crying. He was only seven years old.

My parents arranged my bed, and my suitcases were left at the back of the hostel. There was another long room behind the hostel where all the suitcases were kept. A clothes hanger with four loops was assigned to each student. The suitcases were left underneath these clothes hangers.

At the back of the hostel, there were two doors. These doors took us to the backyard. There was a small path that led to three toilets for our hostel—Evarts Hostel. The open shower and the two large tubs were made out of concrete. This was something very odd to me, as I had never lived in a place where you had to go out for your toilet needs. I always needed to use the toilet in the night, and this worried me straight away.

There was a light switch in front of the back door, but I couldn't see any light bulbs. I returned to my bed and sat there. My parents said good-bye to me, kissed me, and told me to take care. I saw tears in Mummy's eyes, but Dadda was very strong. It was tough, and I felt very empty. I didn't know what to think or expect. I saw my dad's green car leave, and I waited in the verandah for some time, waved them good-bye, and went back in, wiping away my tears.

I continued to sit on my bed until Rajkumar introduced himself as the hostel monitor and said that he was in Grade 7. He told me that we would not have anything to do before dinner, but from next day onward, we would wake up at five forty-five in the morning and go into a set routine. The college bell would ring to wake us up, followed by prayer time. We had half an hour to wash our faces, attend to our toilet needs, and be ready for prayers. There were only three toilets for forty boys. He warned me that it would be a rush. None of the boys were allowed to take a shower in the mornings; that would be done in the evenings.

We were expected to study during a stipulated time. We called these simply "Studies." The morning Studies started after the prayer time at six thirty and ended at seven forty-five when we had breakfast. School started at eight forty-five sharp. We needed to have breakfast and go back to the hostel, get dressed, and go to school.

Rajkumar also emphasized that all the hostels were inside the school and that no one was allowed to go out without the permission of the master in charge. Rajkumar was very kind to explain all this to me, and I had no questions. He must have wondered whether anything had got through to me. It was scary, and I felt a bit helpless. Being eight and a half years old, I missed my parents and family. I cried a bit, but I had no choice. Some of the other boys consoled me and told me that boarding was great fun and I would be enjoying it as time went by.

Around seven thirty that night, we all crossed the college grounds and went to the dining room. That was another warehouse with rows of long tables. There was a piece of metal, possibly from a railway line, hanging in front of the dining room. I asked Rajkumar what that was; he said that it was used to ring the dining room bell. I really couldn't work out exactly how you could ring the bell from this piece of metal.

At 7:42 p.m., someone came out, took a long piece of metal pipe, and had a go at this metal piece. It rang like a bell. His name was Nagamuttu. He had a unique style and looked like he enjoyed having a go at this metal piece. He took back that pipe as though it was made of gold and placed it somewhere.

I thought that it was time for dinner and went inside the dining room. No one followed me; they all stood outside. Ramu, another of the cooks, blasted at me and told me to get out. I said that I was there for dinner. He again blasted me and told me that we were allowed only after the second ring, not the first. Rajkumar hadn't told me that we had two rounds.

I went out and stood close to the door. I was very lonely and had no friends yet. Nagamuttu came out again, took his pipe, and rang the bell again. It was another brilliant performance. I ran in and sat at the first table. Ramu came out and asked me if I was a vegetarian. "No, I hate vegetables. Love meat." I got blasted for the third time and was told that the first two tables were reserved for vegetarians. I was supposed to sit at the third table that was for the younger boys and nonvegetarians.

I immediately ran to the third table and sat there, but everyone else was standing. Nagamuttu rang the bell again, but this time only two rings. I was still seated when the guy next to me asked me to stand up and gave me a dirty look. I stood up when someone from the head table said in a loud voice, "For these and other mercies, we thank you, Lord." I realized that we must thank God before eating, and over the next ten years, this phrase would be repeated thrice a day.

I sat down, and a plate was in front of me with *pittu* on it. It looked like concrete. It was very hard to eat, but I was hungry. There was a bowl with gravy. I started to eat immediately and had almost finished when Ramu came to our table and gave us a piece of fish. I hadn't known that fish was being served, so I had nothing to eat the fish with. All the others at the table paced their eating, as they had known fish was going to be served.

There were about ten older gentlemen in the head table, and one of them was wearing Christian priest clothes, while others were dressed normally. I asked Suthershan if he knew all of them. He said that he had joined the school in January and had some idea. He was of the same age as me and was also from the same hostel. My other neighbour at the table was Diran Sanders. Both of them gave me some information about the gentlemen at the main table. "Bala Arulpragasam, our boarding master, is the college chaplain. The others are boarding masters for other hostels. The man in the middle is our principal, K. Pooranampillai. He is the guy who said the prayer at the beginning. He joins us for dinner every Sunday and on the first night of each term," they explained.

The principal looked very stern and strict. He wore thick glasses. Suthershan and Sanders told me that the food was a bit tough to eat but to hang in there. "You are going to be hungry all the time, and that will force you to like the food." I didn't get what they were talking about but nodded in agreement.

There were two kettles for each table. I took them close to me and poured the coffee into my red plastic cup. I was shocked when there was no coffee inside but just plain water. I asked whether the coffee came after we finished eating. Suthershan laughed and laughed. "*Machchan*, there is no coffee or no tea. There is only water, *machchan*."

I had heard the word *machchan* before. A cousin was always referred to as *machchan*. "Oh, you are my cousin?"

"No, are we?"

"You called me '*machchan*.' Are you my cousin or not? A simple question," I replied. He laughed again and shared the joke with all the boys at the table. I couldn't understand what the fuss was about. Apparently, *machchan* meant mate or friend. I knew that I wouldn't be able to remember the names of all the boys, and now *machchan* could be used to overcome this problem.

Our table was full of Evarts boys, and we became very close. Thanapalan, Wijeyanathan, Kamaleswaran, Maheswaran, Suthershan, Baheerathan, Sri Baskaran, Sanders, and a few others were on our table.

The vegetables that were served were so bad that we used to take them off our plates and put them under the table. We were supposed to eat everything; otherwise, we would have problems with the prefects and the masters.

The first day at school was very interesting. I was assigned to Grade 4C. My class teacher was Miss Arulampalam. I bought a few exercise books, and my parents had bought some textbooks at Poopalasingham Book Depot. I had all of them in a small suitcase made by Ford. It was blue. There were two keys, with one kept inside my big clothes trunk; the other was always inside my pocket.

I didn't know what to expect, other than to go to this class and figure it out. Miss was very kind to me. She took me by the hand and escorted me to my desk. I sat next to Dhayalan. She gave us the timetable. I couldn't believe how regimented it was. School would start at eight forty-five in the morning and finish at three forty-five in the afternoon. There would be eight study periods with a short, fifteen-minute interval and a forty-minute lunch break. I quickly noted that although most periods were each forty minutes long, the first one was always fifty minutes. From that day onward, I hated the first period simply because it was ten minutes longer than others.

I was assigned to Johnstone House. The colour for this house was blue, which matched my suitcase. I was proud of it, as not everyone's suitcases matched their house colours. Dadda and my brothers had also been from Johnstone House.

We came to our first morning interval. Everyone ran to the "tuck shop," but I had no money, so I stayed back. I was invited by some of the boys to play cricket. I was quite excited, as I loved cricket but never played it. We all went to a space close to a building—the Memorial Block. Some of the older boarders lived here. I didn't see any wickets or a turf strip. A boy placed two small suitcases on top of each other, and that became our wickets. He marked twenty-two yards from the suitcases, placed a few pairs of shoes there, and they became the bowling creases. We were ready to go.

Two teams were formed in no time, and our team lost the toss. We were to field. I was hoping to bat and wondered how we could play four innings in fifteen minutes, but this match lasted a full month. We just continued to play as and when we could during the short intervals and at the lunch breaks. I was a terrible fielder and dropped the first catch that came my way. I was quickly dispatched to field directly behind the wicket keeper and at the boundary. We used tennis balls, and I was not sure where the bats and balls came from. We had the full set. It was great fun.

During the lunch break, all the boarders went to the dining room. It was the same routine. Two classic bell ringings by Nagamuttu followed by grace, and we started to eat. This time, I noticed that everyone ate in a hurry. Suthershan was gobbling, saying that we needed to eat fast so that we could continue playing the matches we had started during the short interval. Still, even if we finished our food quickly, we had to wait for everyone on the table to finish theirs. This was another thing that I learnt. Everything was focused on team building.

As I went past the grounds to Evarts Hostel, I saw about thirty matches getting ready to be played in the college grounds and every other vacant space. It was an amazing sight. All the wickets were two small suitcases.

The afternoon, three study periods went fast. I always liked the afternoon sessions because there weren't too many study periods, and one could look forward to the evening. Thus my first day at Grade 4C ended, and I became a Johnian—the name given to all who attended St. John's College.

After school, all the boarders went to their respective boarding houses and then returned to the dining room for tea. There was no bell ringing; we just went into the dining room and had some tea and biscuits. It was a quick, five-minute session. This was not compulsory for all boarders. We then had our daily fun time, which was games.

The first term that ran from January to April was popular for cricket, and we all played cricket during games. Each hostel was provided with bats, tennis balls, and wickets. The second term, which ran from May to August, was popular for athletics and hockey. But we played a great game called *kilithattu*. The third term was popular for football, and each hostel was provided with a football.

After games finished at five forty-five, the college bell would ring, and we went back to our hostels. This was when the boarders took their showers. At Evarts, there was only one shower and two bathtubs. The hostel was divided into four groups named A, B, C, and D. I was in C. (Since I was also in Grade 4C, I wondered whether I would always be a C person.) Groups A and B would shower on Mondays, Wednesdays, and Fridays, while the other two groups bathed on other days. All could bathe on Sundays, when the routine was very different.

During this break of half an hour, you washed yourself and dressed up for the evening. Most would go to the canteen and purchase a cup of tea and a piece of cake. I had no money and was desperate to eat something from the canteen. Rajkumar told me to get some coupons. These were meal tickets that could be used at the tuck shop. They would then charge the value of the tickets to my account that would be paid off by my parents. This was a welcome tip. I immediately wanted coupons but was asked to wait till the next morning to get them from the college office.

The evening Studies promptly started at six fifteen. The Evarts boys went to a classroom close by. It was my first day, and I didn't know what to study. The Tamil language book had a good story at the back called "Ramayanam." I got straight into it and was reading when I felt someone giving a small knock on my head.

I looked up and saw a short man who had woken me up and asked me to concentrate on my Studies. I was glad that he didn't look at what I was reading. Mr. P. S. A. Arulraj worked in the college office and supervised the study sessions for Evarts. He told me that I couldn't sleep during Studies but needed to do my homework and be ready for next day.

I got through my first Studies, and the evening prayers followed. The Christians assembled in a classroom, where a spiritual song was sung, a Bible verse was read, and a small prayer was said. The Hindus and Muslims prayed at their bedsides.

We went to the dining room for our dinner and the same Nagamuttu routine, grace, and dinner. We went back to our hostels, and all the lights at Evarts were off by nine o'clock.

This was a life-changing day for me. I was still lonely and missed my parents, but the day was filled with activities, and I didn't get a chance to relax. I had to quickly get into a strict, disciplined routine. As drifted off to sleep, I just thought of my first day and the routine that would become mine for the next ten years:

05:45 Wake up
06:15 Prayers
06:30 Studies

08:00 Breakfast
08:45 School started: morning session of three study periods

11:10 Short interval

11:25 Midmorning session of two study periods

12:45 Lunch

13:45 Afternoon session of three study periods
15:45 School finished

15:50 Tea
16:00 Games
17:45 Games finished

18:15 Studies
19:45 Prayers
20:00 Dinner
21:00 Lights off for Evarts Hostel

At the end of the first month, the class cricket team was chosen. Nobody had ever mentioned to me that the first month was a trial period for it. I was selected purely because I was a left-arm bowler, as I was the only one who bowled that way. The captain, who was eight years old, wanted a left-arm bowler to spin the opposition out. That was his strategy. I had never bowled in my life. He told me that he had heard of great bowlers like Sobers, who bowled left arm, and that I, too, could easily bowl like him.

It was during one of the short intervals that my first over was clouted for twenty runs and my second for sixteen runs. It was just getting better when we had to return to the classroom. I was fortunate that I had started during the short break and not the luncheon break; otherwise, I would have gone for a lot of runs. I survived and slowly became a team member, although I didn't do very well.

Our boarding master, Rev. Arulpragasam, was very strict. He introduced a lot of activities, trained us to do Christmas plays, and taught us a lot of English songs. The first song that he taught us was "Row, Row, Row Your Boat." He told the selected few to keep this as a secret, as he wanted us to sing at the college function in November.

We had a social event for our hostel in October and played a game called "parcel passing"—you passed the parcel, and whoever held it when the music stopped had to do a predetermined act. I got caught once and had to sing an English song. As I didn't know any other English song, I proudly blurted out "Row, Row, Row Your Boat," thus spoiling it for Rev, who had had big plans for it. He was furious. He told me that I would be punished and asked me to his house every evening to write a line saying, "I will not disobey my teacher." I had to write this one hundred times for five consecutive days.

We were all very young, and Rev was mostly very kind to us. He knew we were very homesick, as our parents lived far from Jaffna. His wife took an active role in our lives. She would periodically inspect our boarding house and made sure that we kept it very clean. She would ensure that all of us were keeping our dirty clothes in a linen bag.

Fourth grade went by in a flash. This was the year that made me settle down. I had many times felt really homesick. It was very difficult to get used to the food, the bed, the toilets, and the showers. The daily routine was brutal, and you couldn't be late for anything. The college bell and the dining room bell kept us in check. I missed my parents dearly. There were so many nights when I cried in my bed thinking of them, wanting to go back.

I came to St. John's during the second term of 1968. I had spent the previous term at Trinity College, Kandy, and was boarded at the vice principal Mr. Sahayam's house. I was so homesick then that I used to write to my parents asking them to take me home. I kept writing that I wanted to sleep in their bed and missed them badly. My parents felt sorry for me and took me off Trinity College and admitted me here, where my brothers were already boarding. The challenge was that Jaffna was two hundred and fifty miles away from Hatton, where my parents lived, compared to the forty-three miles from Kandy. I basically went further away from them, but at least my brothers were here.

I enjoyed games time and quickly got acquainted with all the sports that were available. The senior boys played hockey, and Under 15s played cricket during the second term. I was too young for that and kept playing *kilithattu*.

The college athletic meet usually took place during the second term. As I was in the lower school, we had a different athletic meet. I was part of Johnstone House team. I was selected for the lime-and-spoon race. Fifth grade boys were the seniors among the lower school, and I had to listen to them. I was told to hold the spoon tightly and run to the finishing line with the lime on top of my spoon.

The starter blew the whistle, and everyone started running. I, too, ran. I came fourth. I was disappointed but was proud to have beaten six others until the house captain slapped me on the back of my shoulder and asked me to show him the lime. I turned and saw my lime lying on the ground at the starting line. I was disqualified. My first race was a huge disappointment.

I was not selected for anything but was assigned to glucose duty. This was great. I had to run after the athletes after they finished the race and give them glucose. I was also supposed to give them glucose before the race. (While the race was on, I ate most of it.) This allowed me to meet all the Johnstone House athletes. Johnstone House came in last.

At the boarding house, we all got on fine. I was slowly forming good friendships. We were getting used to the food and the routine, and we were beginning to enjoy the boarding life. I always keenly waited for the weekends. On Saturdays, there would be Studies in the morning and another one-hour study session after breakfast. After that, we would run straight to the ground and play cricket. I was slowly getting better at my left-arm leg breaks. I was told where to bowl or not to bowl by the senior captain, Rajkumar. He was a fast bowler and bowled very good bouncers with a tennis ball.

We played a match against Thompson Hostel. We were thrashed by an innings and seventy-five runs. I was slaughtered for seventy runs in four overs and scored eleven and four when I batted. The lime-and-spoon race, and now the cricket match—both ended disastrously.

On Saturday nights, we had something called a "meeting." Here, we sat down and did various activities: singing, speeches, and storytelling. We had to elect a president and a secretary. Every Saturday, they would preside over a meeting where the secretary would read the minutes of the previous Saturday's meeting, which had to be approved by the audience. Three people would then sing a song, each followed by three people giving short speeches. At the end, we would eagerly await the storyteller.

The first meeting was good fun. The singing was shocking, and the speeches were so bad that they put me to sleep. The storyteller was Sugumar. He laid out the scene of a house with a father, a mother, and two kids. The parents went shopping in the night and left the two kids of eight and six alone. The children were scared, as the house had no lights. Somehow, a ghost and a snake had gotten in there. As he was relating that, he slowly switched off the lights and kept a torch under his chin.

Within a few minutes, all of us were screaming and crying with Wijeyanathan, shivering and howling. I was holding on to him and screaming too. We were in this dark room and could only see Sugumar's face with the torch under his chin. It was terribly scary. We then heard someone coming into the room, and we shouted even louder.

The person who came in switched on the lights and started hitting Sugumar on the head. It was Mr. Panchalingham. He lived close to Evarts. He shouted at Sugumar for making us all scared and asked him to stop the story. We were still shouting and crying. Mr. Panchalingham then calmed us down and told us to sing a few more songs and left the room. We were all so angry with Sugumar, but he had enjoyed making us scared.

Sundays were different. No one was allowed to play at the college grounds. It was a complete rest day. We had to go to church twice: seven in the morning and five in the evening. It was compulsory to attend Sunday school as well. This was the first time we came into contact with anyone outside the school. At our Sunday school, we would get a few girls too. They were from our sister school, Chundikuli Girls' College.

Boarders were encouraged to write a letter to their parents on Sundays. I had to write the letter and then give it to Ranjit

Anna. I didn't know what to write. I used to write about the trees and the grass around the hostel but hardly wrote anything about myself.

Sunday dinners were special. Every Tuesday and Thursday, we were served beef but no chicken or pork. But on Sundays, we got mutton curry. Our principal would attend the dinner and say the grace.

Early July, Ranjit Anna told me that we were going to visit our grandparents in Uduvil for the weekend. This was so exciting, as two months had passed, and I hadn't gone out even once. He told me to pack a few pieces of clothing in my small suitcase and be ready after school on Friday. I was really looking forward to it. Mummy was coming from Hatton, as my aunt, Ranee Acca, had had a baby girl. I was ecstatic. I missed my parents so much and found it very difficult to adjust.

I ran from my classroom to Evarts, collected my small suitcase, ran back, and stood in front of Williams Hall. My brothers joined me, and we went out of school. We passed Bastiampillai Junction and waited for the bus to Jaffna. We then took another bus to Uduvil. I was very excited to see Mummy and ran in and kissed her. I had two younger brothers, Delano and Ruki; they were five and one. We were a family with five boys. I went inside the house and saw my little cousin, Gita. She was only ten days old. She was very sweet. Her brother, Suthan, was two years old.

This was my grandparents' house down Malvam Lane. They looked after me when I did my early schooling at Uduvil Girls College before I went to Trinity. They both gave us all big hugs, and we were so happy to eat my grandmother's cooking. We called her Ammachchi and my grandfather Aiyah. Their maid, Mary, helped them with the cooking.

We had so much to talk about, and we had a superb meal sitting around the big dining table with Aiyah at the head of the table. Ammachchi always stood next to us while we ate and made sure we got served all the special food that she had made for us. She would eat last.

After dinner, we sat around and chatted. We talked about all kinds of things. My brothers were telling them everything that was happening at school while I just sat and listened. Ranee Acca played some Jim Reeves songs on the big Grundig machine. It was a big box, and she played her records on them. We were served a glass of *lakspray* (hot milk) before we slept. I saw Mummy, Ranee Acca, and her husband, Deva Uncle, together with my grandparents sitting on the verandah and chatting.

There were four rooms in the house. The three boys slept on the mats in the main hall. Mary laid out the mats and gave us pillows and some bedsheets to cover ourselves with. She then switched off the lights. I had a great dinner and fell asleep very fast.

I was awakened suddenly and saw a lot of people running up and down. Mummy looked very upset, and Ranee Acca was crying. I saw a dark green, long car parked outside. I saw Ammachchi being carried to the car. She looked very sleepy. We were asked to move out and to go inside the room. I ran to the front window and looked out. It was a terrible sight. That was the last time I saw Ammachchi alive. I didn't know what was happening until Wijit Anna told me that she had fallen ill during the night and had to be taken to the hospital.

That day was very lonely. All were worried about Ammachchi. We just played outside without knowing exactly what was happening. That night, we had dinner and went to bed. I heard some noise and I saw Mummy dressing up, wearing her saree. I got up, and she told me that Ammachchi was very sick. The hospital had asked her and Aiyah to go there. She had tears in her eyes, and I knew she was trying to hold them back. A blue Austin A40 came and took both of them.

A few hours later, another uncle of mine, Babu Uncle, came rushing into the house and started moving and rearranging the furniture, leaving a big space in the middle of our sitting room. I was playing outside, trying to climb a tree, when I heard Ranee Acca crying out loudly. I ran inside, and she was holding another person, Rasu Aunty, and crying uncontrollably. I didn't know what was happening. Mary was crying, and my brothers were crying as well. Why were all crying so loudly and heavily?

Mary held my hand and told me that Ammachchi had died. It was a terrible feeling, as I never had a chance to say good-bye. I cried a lot alone, as Mummy and Aiyah were still at the hospital. It was the first time I experienced a death and losing someone so close. She was a lovely lady, very pretty and graceful. She was always immaculately dressed. She was born in 1905 and had been only sixty-three years old.

We saw a car coming in and ran outside. I first saw Aiyah getting down from the car. He was holding the tree in the garden and was sobbing softly, "My princess is gone…my princess is gone." He kept on repeating this. They had been meant for each other from their teens.

Ranee Acca ran to him and held him tight and cried. Mummy got down and slowly brought them into the house, but she was also crying. I watched Ammachchi's body being carried in, and she was placed on a bed in the middle of the sitting room. She was asleep, and her hands were clasped in front as if she was praying. I went close to her and kissed her forehead. Deva Uncle and Suthan also kissed her and were crying. It was a house full of people crying.

Rev. Jeyasingham said a small prayer and then started discussing the funeral details with someone. It was all happening so fast. Mummy told me that Dadda was driving to attend the funeral. Within one hour, the house was full of people. Everyone who came into the house would first kiss Aiyah and then Mummy, Ranee Acca, and Deva Uncle. They cried very loudly when they kissed them and then paid their respects to my grandmother. Some close relatives sat inside the house while others sat outside.

A lot of chairs were brought in, and each chair had a mark, "Barton Mather," since they were hired from him. My grandparents were well known in the area, and they were from a strong Christian family. They belonged to the Church of South India (CSI). Ammachchi's death brought a lot of people to the house. By that evening, there must have been over five hundred people visiting it. All kinds of people came in, and I didn't know a single one of them.

Everyone howled and cried. They shouted and cried. They said a lot of nice things about Ammachchi and cried. Each time someone cried, I cried too. In between, I played outside, but as someone came into the house, I would run to see what he or she would do and then cried when they cried. The crying operation was sort of fun to watch. Each person had a different technique. There were a few who were seated behind Aiyah. They joined in and cried whenever someone came in and consoled Mummy and Ranee Acca. This operation was called *opparri*. They used a very high-pitched voice to cry and uttered a lot of words, mostly praising my grandmother.

I was climbing the front tree again when the gate opened and the green Morris Minor drove in. I knew it was my Dadda. I quickly came down the tree and ran towards him. He hugged all of us. Dadda was not a very emotional person, but I knew he was very disturbed. He kissed us and came into the house. My mum stood up and went towards him. She cried so loudly that I was worried for her. They both hugged each other, but only my mother kept crying. I was so happy to see my dad. He then walked towards us and sat with us. We were talking to him, and he was carrying Ruki. I was not interested in Ammachchi anymore but sat next to my Dadda and held his hand. Mummy was busy with the visitors. Her brothers, Walter Mama and Ranjan Mama, also came in. They were so upset, and it was very sad to see them like that.

The term ended in August, and we got our vacation. This was my first vacation since I had joined college. I was waiting to go back to my parents, although I had just seen them in July during Ammachchi's funeral. I was still very homesick and was really looking forward to going back to Hatton.

On the day the school term ended, the classes finished by midday. We all got our marks from the term tests. I did well in English and got eighty-five marks, but all the other marks were pretty average—around sixty. This was not bad, as I got the overall grading of Good. There were five gradings applied based on the average marks. The top end is Honours, followed by Good, Pass, Fail, and Bad Fail. I was quite pleased that I was able to get Good. The school report got posted to our homes during the holidays.

After lunch, we took a car arranged by Aiyah back to his house. After the death of Ammachchi, he had moved to Chavakachcheri. He was living together with Deva Uncle and Ranee Acca and their two kids. This was our native place. They were now living at 7, Dutch Road, Chava, just behind Drieberg College. My parents owned this house. They had built it in 1965.

The car picked us up at three. My brothers seemed to know the driver, Sathasivam. He was wearing a green-and-yellow sarong, a bit bulky, and was chewing something all the time. He drove a dark green Austin Somerset car. He was always smiling. He took our bags and placed them nicely in the car boot. Our trunks were left behind at the hostel, as we would not need all our clothes during the holidays. My brother was a bit upset. He thought I had a lot of dirty clothes—and I did.

We went over Navatkuli Bridge, passed the Kaithaddy Junction, and then to Chava. This was my first ever trip to Chava. We went inside the house and gave Aiyah a hug and a kiss and did the same to Ranee Acca and Deva Uncle. We had *vadai* and some Chinese rolls for our tea. We stayed late that night and had a good chat. We played carom and a word game called Lexicon. My two cousins were still so young. I loved playing with Suthan, tickling him and making funny faces to him. He would laugh a lot. Gita was still a baby, and I was too scared to carry her.

Ranee Acca, with the help of Mary, always cooked lovely meals. This time it was *pittu*, mutton curry, and sambal. I had the habit of mixing some sugar into it. Aiyah warned me, "Chooty, be careful with your sugar. You might get diabetes." (I was called "Chooty" at home.)

"What is that, Aiyah?"

My brothers were laughing when Ranee Acca intervened. "Diabetes? This boy is only eight years old! Let him enjoy his sugar!"

Next day, we got up very late. I was very relieved not to hear the college bell. I went over to our neighbours' house. The first house belonged to Mummy's cousin, Kamala Aunty. They had two kids—Ranji and Viji. There were two other kids, Ananthan and Vathani, who were Kamala Aunty's sister's—Leela Aunty's—children. They had come there for the holidays. Pushpa Aunty lived next to them, and her son, Nihal, joined us too.

We played something called *dinkiri dinkiri*. It was a hide-and-seek game but had some twists, with a tin full of stones. The aim was to capture this tin and shout, *"Dinkiri, dinkiri!"*

That evening, we took the mail train to Polgahawela, and then from there, we had to take another train to Hatton. The train left Chava around seven forty-five, and we were at Polgahawela by five in the morning.

Ranee Acca had cooked a nice dinner of string hoppers, *sothi*, and beef curry for the trip. Ranjit Anna woke me up when we passed Vavuniya, and we had our dinner. It was still very dark when we got down at Polgahawela. The connecting train to Hatton, Udarata Menike, came only at eight in the morning, and that would take us to Hatton around noon.

We could see our house at Fruit Hill when we approached Hatton Station. It was a great feeling. Dadda picked us up, and we then spent a month with the family. We spent most of the time playing outside, going to the local river, and watching a few movies.

There were three cinemas in Hatton. The Princess always showed English movies, while Wijitha and Liberty showed Tamil movies. We joined our parents when they went shopping. Ranjit Anna got a Camy wristwatch. We attended Sunday services at our local Anglican church—Christ Church, Dickoya. We had a lot of fun. It was very sad when we had to leave our home to go back to school. We had no choice.

We followed the same routine in reverse order. We changed trains at Polgahawela and ended back at Chava. We arrived in the morning, went to Aiyah's, and left with Sathasivam to go to school. We had to be in the hostels the day before the school reopened for the third term: September to December.

This would be the final term, and I needed to do well. Based on our term tests, we got promoted to the next grade. Every grade had three classes—A, B, and C. The bright students would be in A. I wanted to be there. I continued to find studying very hard and fell asleep every time I opened my books.

One day after school, our hostel monitor, Rajkumar, summoned us to the front of Evarts Hostel. He looked very, very serious. He was only eleven, but he looked like a big man. "We need to win. We need to be positive. This is what Norman Vincent Peale wrote."

What is he talking about? Who is this Norman? I thought. I was very confused and looked around to see if others were. Maheswaran was munching something and was drawing circles on the ground with his toes. Thanapalan was doing something with his fingers and making faces. I was standing next to Sivasothy and asked him what this entire lecture was about. It was a lecture about positive thinking by an eleven-year-old to those younger than him. Sivasothy made a gesture with his palm to say that he would explain to me later.

I continued to listen. Rajkumar rambled on and on and never told us what this was about. I was annoyed, as he was taking our games time. We were now approaching forty-five minutes of this monologue, and at the end, Rajkumar made us understand what he was talking about. There would be a Boarders' Day in two months, and we needed to prepare ourselves. I had never heard of this day and continued to be confused.

I caught up with Sivasothy and asked him about it. He told me that there would be a series of events, including drama, dialogue, singing, sports, and a fast-eating competition. These events would last for one week, eventually ending on a Saturday—the Boarders' Day. We were supposed to work on the drama, dialogue, and a hostel song. He told me that it was very good fun and I must get fully involved in it.

The great thing about the Boarders' Day was that there would be a series of cricket matches between the hostels. We were also allowed to practice our dramas and songs during the Studies. This was a tremendous incentive for me to actively participate, as I simply hated these Studies.

Rajkumar picked a drama called *Raja Raja Cholan*. It was about kings and queens. It was a very serious drama, and I had never read that story. My role was to hold a fan for the king, who was Rajkumar himself. That was it. I did nothing during the practices but pretend to hold a fan over the king. No words said, no movement of my body, but just stood still with a fan. I didn't have a clue about this story of kings and queens, but the conversations were made of different songs from Tamil films.

We used the song "Kannan Varuvan" from a Tamil movie, *Panchavarnakilli*, and created the hostel song from it. We changed the words to describe Evarts boys. I was not selected to be part of the team to sing. That was a bit disappointing.

I thought I needed to impress my eleven-year-old seniors with my singing. I crafted a plan. I waited till the senior boys went to the toilet. I then sang as loudly as possible. I did that while

I brushed my teeth until one of them told me to be careful, as I could swallow the toothbrush. No one was impressed, and I abandoned the idea. I was now left with only one thing to do for the Boarders' Day: holding the fan for the king!

Before the Sunday dinner, we would sit on the college grounds and have a chat. Sivasothy took me aside with Thanapalan and gave us another lecture. He told us that we were the juniors, but we were the future of Evarts. He encouraged us to participate with full energy at the Boarders' Day. I was a bit puzzled, as I didn't know what energy to display holding that stupid fan. He explained that Boarders' Day was an opportunity to prove that we were growing up.

There were seven hostels, but I didn't know that yet. The baby hostel was Evarts, and then Thompson. Once you passed eighth grade, you got sent to the Memorial Block, which had four hostels: Dr. Rajasingham, Handy, Alison, and Crossette. After one year in Crossette, you went to Fleming, where you would end up taking the advanced-level exams. For us at Evarts, our main rival was Thompson. Dr. Rajasingham fought it out with Handy while Alison and Crossette challenged Fleming.

I got it! We had to beat Thompson at every competition. But there was a catch to it. That was only for sporting events, while all the other events were open to all. Sivasothy pumped both of us up, and I shouted, "Come on!" a few times.

Over the next six weeks, we had tremendous fun. We had drama practices. We played practice cricket matches. The singers were working on the hostel song secretly. My involvement was very little. I was to hold the fan for the king and play as the number-eleven batsman for our cricket team. I was still considered to be that star left-arm spinner who was supposed to turn the ball on muddy wickets, and with a tennis ball. I was going to be the trump card! How wrong were they!

The Boarders' Day week began. Our cricket match started on a Wednesday evening. We went and had our tea. The Evarts cricket team was under strict instructions from Rajkumar. We were told to drink water and eat nothing so no one had any tummy issues. I cleaned my hands from the elbow downward and cleaned my fingers and nails. This was the way left-arm bowlers prepared for cricket matches. I was the eight-year-old sensation that was going to be used as a trump card to beat the mighty Thompson Hostel. Yes, David was getting ready to take on eleven Goliaths. "Come on, come on!" I kept shouting before the match. Rajkumar told me to shut up, as I was upsetting others.

We won the toss and batted. This match was to be played over a four-hour period. Our openers put on twelve runs before both of them were bowled. We were quickly six wickets down for twenty-two. Enter Thanapalan. He slammed two fours and a six while three wickets fell on the other side. Forty-six for nine. Enter me. I had a bat that came up to my shoulder, and I found it very difficult to hold. Thanapalan told me to focus hard, to put my head down and block the ball. He was confident that we would pass fifty. He believed that it would be a decent score. "Come on, Come on," I kept on muttering. "Come on, Come on."

He walked towards me and told me to shut up and to put my head down and block the ball. "Okay, *machchan*, head down, but come on." I was not going to let go of my own "come on."

The first ball came at a terrific speed towards me and bounced. I had been asked to keep my head down, and I did. Before I could blink, the ball hit me in the middle of my face. I was bleeding from the nose. I looked up at Thanapalan. "You told me to put my head down, *machchan*. I did, but this ball hit my nose."

He encouraged me to take it for the team and bat again. I was now playing for the team. "Okay, come on."

Next ball took all three of my stumps and cleaned me up. I was out without a score but lasted two balls. I was playing as a left-arm, sensational bowler. I was not bothered about the batting. We were all out for forty-six runs. It lasted twenty-two minutes.

I had a chance to bowl when they were twenty-two for no loss. My first three balls were dispatched for three sixes and the next two for two fours. Match over. My only over cost twenty-six runs. I made sure that I shouted, "Come on!" after every ball, but it was to no avail. We lost badly. We shook hands and went back to Evarts. Rajkumar told us to forget it and focus on the other Boarders' Day activities. The only thing left was to fan the king!

Over the past few weeks, we had added the final touches for the drama and the hostel song. We were eagerly anticipating this Boarders' Day, as for some of us, it was for the first time. I didn't know what to expect.

I was doing my studies reasonably well but continually fell asleep on the study table. I kept thinking of my parents and found it difficult not to be at home, but I ploughed through. There were times when I would go to bed counting the number of days before I could go back to Hatton for our holidays. I would sit in bed and think of the nice food we got at home compared to the stuff at the boarding school. I would think of all that and cry, but I never shared that with anyone.

Sivasothy was Rajkumar's sidekick, and he was organizing everything. Rajkumar focused on the main things, like coaching the actors and singers. He kept quoting Norman Vincent Peale. We really looked up to him.

The best day of my life arrived—a day that perhaps changed my life forever. It was a day when I experienced both victory and defeat. It was a day when I enjoyed being at the boarding school and wanted to be there forever.

The Boarders' Day actually started on the Friday evening before and ended on Saturday. On that Friday after school, we went back to Evarts. Rajkumar had had his evening shower; he was wearing a red sarong with a white vest. He sat on his bed, and we were all standing around him. This time, he quoted heavily from Winston Churchill: "We must win at all costs." We were the babies, but he wanted us to beat them all. Everyone said something, and I shouted, "Come on, come on!"

We all got dressed and went to the dining room. The opening event was the fast eaters' competition. We fielded our guy, Thevasenathipathy, whose nickname was Villungas. He was only ten years old but a big, fat boy. That was why he was selected, as we thought he could eat a lot, and fast. Every other hostel sent two competitors, but Villungas was our sole guy. They had to eat a pound of bread, a quarter pound of meat, and two bananas, and drink one huge, plastic cup filled with water. We all stood out and watched them. I was thinking how nice it would be to eat this food and decided one day that I should enter this event.

Satchi from Alison won. Villungas took a long time and started coughing. He was choking and had to be stopped.

We all went into the dining room for our dinner. We had lovely food—fried rice and brinjal curry with mutton. We had orange juice instead of water. We had an enjoyable dinner. We wore our best clothes, and the dining room was very colourful and cheerful.

The masters were very relaxed, and no one talked about Studies. This was the beginning of a day of activities that brought sheer enjoyment and pleasure.

After dinner, we went to the main hall—Robert Williams Hall. While we were at dinner, the hall had been filled with a lot of people—mostly day scholars, parents, teachers, and their families. They had come to watch the drama competition. I was shocked to see so many people there.

Each drama had to run for fifteen minutes. Evarts was given the fifth slot. I had to wear my costume to be the fan bearer, and it involved a saree that had been converted to the kind of trousers that old kings in India wore. Rajkumar and Sivasothy had hired all these costumes, and I just had to wear it. I wore a vest above the trousers and shoes made out of cardboard.

We were to go to the back of the stage after the third drama, and someone would then dress us up. The first three dramas were great. They attracted a lot of laughter, as they were hilarious. I made sure I went behind the stage at the correct time and got quickly dressed. We missed the fourth play, but I heard a lot of laughter from the crowd. This made me think of our drama—*Raja Raja Cholan*. It was too serious, I thought.

The bell rang for the fifth play, and it was ours. The first scene had the king seated and ordering someone to bring his court jester. I had to stand behind him, waving this stupid fan made out of cardboard and attached to a six-foot, wooden pole. The dialogue was mixed with words and songs. I felt so bored, and I was yawning. It was past my bedtime. I kept looking at the crowd and could see my brothers. I was getting very distracted.

Suddenly, I heard a big noise and saw the king on the floor. I had hit the king with the flagpole. I had dropped it, and he fell down to the ground. He quickly got up, and I saw a big, red mark on his head. He muttered for me to move back and continued with the drama. It was so boring. I decided that from there on, we must always have a comedy drama and nothing else.

After all the dramas were finished, there was a short interval of twenty minutes when the three judges met to decide on the first three places and an award for Best Actor's Prize. We had no chance and didn't win anything. We were not even mentioned, except the main judge joked that the fan carrier had been a bit tired. That was the end of Friday. It set the scene for next day. We went to bed late but had to wake up very early and be ready for the opening ceremony. I kept dreaming of my talents as a fan carrier.

The college bell rang. It was a very chilly day, slightly cold. Rajkumar, who still had a big, red mark on his forehead, woke me up. We all wore white shirts with blue shorts for the official opening ceremony. It was held in front of the dining room inside the college grounds. There was a flagpole, and our college flag was nicely folded and tied to the pole.

Everyone, including the cooks, was there. The principal and the boarding masters stood in front. A group of ten students then went forward and sang the Boarders' Day song. It was a very touching song about how we enjoy ourselves, form friendships, and live harmoniously. The song was titled "*Ellorum Kondaduvom,*" meaning "let us all celebrate." The president of the boarders union, a senior student from Fleming Hostel, spoke, and then the principal wished us all well. That was the start of that amazing day.

Throughout the day, we had football matches, *kilithattu* competition, a slow cycle race, and a dialogue and a singing competition. During the tea break, there were two more competitions. First, there was the "hit the pot" competition. A pot with water was tied at the top of a large pole. The competitors were blindfolded and given long sticks. They were then taken about one hundred yards away and let loose. They had to make it to the pole and hit the pot and break it. It was a fascinating event, and you sometimes found competitors hitting each other. It was followed by the fancy-dress competition, where people dressed up in funny clothes and did funny acts.

The competition among us was fierce. Our sole aim was to beat Thompson Hostel in the sporting events. We knew in other competitions that it would be hard to beat other, senior hostels. I was so overjoyed when we beat Thompson Hostel in *kilithattu*. We lost all the matches in every other sport, and that was very disappointing. The day ended with a football match between Fleming and a combined team from Alison and Crossette Hostels.

After the match, we went back to our hostels to dress up for dinner. The dinner was held on the college grounds with lovely food—mutton curry again, boiled egg, and fried rice. All three meals were great, and we enjoyed the food very much. We knew we would be going back to the same, old food the next day. During the dinner, prizes were distributed to the winners of the various competitions. The president spoke and thanked all for participating fully and then invited his wife to distribute the prizes. We got few prizes, but we were the babies, and no one expected us to win a lot. However, we applauded very loudly when we went to collect the *kilithattu* prize.

The dinner was over in no time. We then sat around and sang a lot of songs and danced. The boarding masters, too, joined in and sang with us. It was very nice to see them relaxed and enjoying things.

That was the best day of my life. I was so happy, and I thought that at least for the Boarders' Day's sake, I must stay on. My outlook on boarding life changed dramatically. I saw everyone enjoying, helping each other, and forming new friendships. I even saw the teachers and the principal relax.

I got promoted to Grade 5A, under Mrs. Thangarajah. This pleased me, as it meant that I had done reasonably well. She was a sweet lady and wore the saree by tucking a piece of it behind her back. It looked like a horse's tail. She was very nice to me and helped me settle down in this new class. I made new friends: Uthayakumar, Benjamin, Kathirkamanathan, Sethukavalar, Rajeswaran, Marino Mahilrajan, Nadanakumar, Nadesakumar, and D. S. Ratnarajah, to name a few.

Year 1969 was very memorable for me, as I truly became a full boarder. I participated in all activities and was notorious for being very naughty. One day, our hostel master called me to his house. "Sinniah, your clothes are a disgrace—you are not clean, and I can't have you go to school like this." My trunk was then kept at his house, and he made sure that I had clean clothes every day.

Next day, when I went to collect a fresh set of clothes, I met Alphonsus and Sanders. They had also been asked to keep their clothes there. The three of us became notorious for keeping dirty clothes and wearing them to school. I was always running around playing sports and making my clothes dirty. I was given my first nickname: *Oothai Sinniah*. *Oothai* meant "dirty."

We had rest time after lunch on Saturdays and Sundays. We hardly slept or rested. We were very restless, especially the three of us. We decided we must do something seriously stupid. We took a pair of scissors and cut all the hair in and around our eyes. We looked so stupid. Someone had informed Rev, our hostel master, about our action. He came barging down the hostel, took three of us out, and punished us. It took about a month and a half to grow our hair back.

I joined the Cub Scout movement. Miss Thambirajah and Miss Arulampalam were in charge. It was very easy at first, but hard work later on. We had to go for Cubs meetings, listen to a few lectures, and then build something with wooden poles and ropes. I hated hard, physical work. I was not a very good cub.

But it was fun, and I met a different set of boys. Once a year, we had a jamboree at Old Park, and cubs from all over Jaffna were there. Our unit was called 2nd Jaffna, meaning that we were the second Cubs unit to be established in Jaffna.

When you joined the Cubs movement, you got a lovely uniform. I particularly liked the cap. It was beautiful. I decided to wear it to play a cricket match. It was played opposite the middle school teachers' room. I looked very impressive. I saw Miss Thambirajah rushing out of the staff room. She came straight for me, pinched me hard just above my hip, and shouted at me. She kept pinching me and told me that the cap should not be worn for sports and could only be worn for Cubs activities.

The cubs took an active part in welcoming the chief guest at the college prize-giving. We would all stand in a circle, and then the chief guest would be brought inside it. We would kneel down and shout, "Akela, we will do our best!" I just loved shouting this.

The Cub Scouts participated in the "chip-a-job" programme. We would visit various houses around our school to do small odd jobs for them and earn some money for the Cubs movement. I collected money by washing cars, cutting small trees, and watering the gardens. In one place, the lady of the house wanted me to polish her husband's shoes. I did it, but I couldn't make them shine. I used a lot of my spit and rubbed. She was very happy with my work and gave me three rupees. I collected around twenty rupees in my first attempt. I was the lowest contributor.

Fifth grade was the final year of lower school before we got promoted to the middle school. Almost all the activities in the school were done separately for lower school from the rest of the school. I actively participated in all lower school activities but never excelled in one. But I built good friendships in my class and at Evarts. The boarding life was becoming fun, and we rarely missed our parents anymore.

Mrs. Thangarajah and Mr. Thuraisamy got together and organized a one-day trip. We paid ten rupees each. It was very exciting to see the real Jaffna. There were about eighty students, and we assembled in front of the college gate. Two buses were arranged to pick us up. Esty and Co. owned these buses locally. Our college always used their buses for picnics and to take us to various events. They were old but comfortable buses and could hold up to fifty people. We went to see numerous places: the glass factory, the Palali airport, the Old Dutch Fort, and Keerimalai.

Last, we went to Delft by boat. This was one of the most memorable and scariest experiences. The boat ride took only fifteen minutes, but as we were nearing the shore, the boat I was in capsized, and all of us fell into the water. None of us had life jackets, so we just frantically held on to the boat. Sir (which is what we called our teachers) was on the boat with us, and he quickly helped us all get back. The water was not that deep; it may have been about five feet. But we were less than ten years old, with an average height of four feet six. It was a hair-raising experience.

We were all completely wet but were glad to be safe. The teachers decided to abandon the trip and took us back to school.

I performed decently in my studies then, and my grades were always Good. I got promoted from lower school to the middle school and was assigned to Grade 6A. Our class teacher was Miss Thambiah. She was very quiet but stern and strict. She taught us English and history. This was the year when subjects like history, geography, mathematics, and general sciences were introduced. These, together with English, Tamil, Christianity, and social studies formed the set of subjects taught in the middle school. I liked mathematics and geography but hated all other subjects, especially history and science.

Our holidays were always spent in Hatton, and we followed the same routine of going to Aiyah's at Chava and then going through Polgahawela to Hatton by train. During one of the holidays, I joined the Young Timers Club that was run by the *Sunday Times*. Your name got printed in the paper if you joined it. I wanted to see my name get printed. The following Sunday, I grabbed the paper and was so thrilled to see my name. That Sunday, they ran a competition where you needed to draw a basket with fruits. Mummy, who was a great artist, helped me to draw this, and we entered the competition. She did most of the drawing and painting, and I just did the borders. I won the contest and was awarded a small suitcase. I had to collect it from the store, Mohamedali Abdulali, next to Ranee theatre. I kept it next to my trunk.

We were required to lock our suitcases and trunk. I kept all my valuables in my small suitcase and locked that only. As I've said, I carried the small key in my pocket. I had this bad habit of putting things in my mouth—pencils and erasers, and sometimes, I kept this small key in my mouth, too. One day, I swallowed the key by accident. I was not that concerned but casually mentioned it to Ranjit Anna. He panicked.

"What? You swallowed a key?"

"Yes."

"What?"

"Yes, I swallowed a small key. What is the problem?"

"Aren't you worried?"

"No. I've got the duplicate key to open my suitcase."

He was shocked and got Deva Uncle to take me to get an X-ray done. They couldn't find the key and assumed that I must have passed the key out with my bowels!

Rev was transferred to a church in Batticaloa. We now got a new hostel master, Major Param Selvarajah. He had a lot of daughters and one son, Michael, who was my classmate. It was a welcome change, as we were now getting a chance to meet some girls. Major quickly established himself with us. He was an old boy of St. John's and knew some of my uncles and aunts. He was very jovial and had a very relaxed attitude towards managing the hostel. My trunk was now back with me, and I didn't need to go to him to collect my clothes every day. My nickname continued to be "Oothai Sinniah."

My birthday—September 19—was always during the school term. We rarely spent our birthdays with our families. Mummy would send us a cake and some toffees to distribute to my hostel and classmates. On the eighteenth, I was asked to go to the office, as there was a parcel for me. I knew it would be a cake but was surprised to find that this one was in the shape of a key. I collected the cake after school and took it back to Evarts. As soon as I walked into the hostel, all my friends pounced on it, and before I could even eat one piece, the cake was finished. It was a huge cake, and I was happy to entertain my friends.

Next day, my two brothers met me and wished me well for my birthday. "Where are our pieces?"

"What pieces?"

"Cake! What else?" Wijit Anna was getting angry.

I had never read the letter in which Mummy instructed me to give them a few pieces of cake. "The cows ate it."

"What?"

"The cows that were roaming behind Evarts came in and ate it. Stupid Ravindran. He was supposed to keep the doors locked."

"Oh, really? Don't just lie to us."

Ranjit Anna gave me a knock on my head and joined Wijit Anna on the way back to their hostels. They knew I was lying and were seriously disappointed.

Our monitor, Arunagirinathar, informed us that some of us would need to move to Thompson Hostel. I was hoping that my name would be called, as I was now a senior guy at Evarts, having been there for two years. My name was one of them, and I got transferred to Thompson Hostel immediately. While I was excited, I also felt very sad, as I had had so much fun in this baby hostel.

Mr. Panchalingham's house was next to Evarts, and I mentioned to him that I was going to Thompson. He warned me not to get too excited, as those who went to Thompson needed to go for extra Studies after dinner. This I hadn't known, and my enthusiasm was quickly dampened.

A few friends helped me to carry my trunk and my little suitcase to Thompson, and I was welcomed by Vipul Arasaratnam, who was Thompson monitor. I had a bed next to his room.

While I was at Thompson, our hostel master, Mr. N. E. Jeyasingham, had a heart attack and died. He had three sons, and they were all at St. John's. I knew all of them and played cricket and football with them. His body was kept at Williams Hall, and the funeral was held the next day. That was the first funeral in the college premises that I witnessed.

Vipul Anna left college in April. Our new hostel master, Mr. Jeya Thevathasan, moved into the room that had been occupied by Vipul Anna. He was a lovely man. He was very young, energetic, jovial, and very kind. He introduced us to hockey, and we started playing it during our games time.

The Third XI hockey team was formed, and Sir was our first coach. We had nine players from Thompson Hostel. We played a few matches and lost all of them. Thevathasan master had a serious influence over us.

My classroom was inside Figg Hall, where sixth and seventh grade were located. I was walking towards my class when Ehan came running and told me that someone in my family had died and that he was very sorry. I had not heard of anything. I dismissed the news and moved on. I thought perhaps Aiyah was sick, and this guy was just blabbering. I was in my class when Miss called me up and told me that my grandmother had died. I told her that my grandmother had died two years earlier and that it would be difficult for her to die again, as she was buried in a cemetery in Chava. She looked at me in total surprise. "How many grandmothers do you have?"

"One dead. One living."

"Then the living one has died. Can't you work out this simple issue?" I realized that it must be my father's mother, Pappamma. I was a bit embarrassed and asked her whether it was my father's mother. "I don't know your family to know which grandmother is living and which one is dead, but one died yesterday." She sounded furious. She rarely got upset, but she was this time.

I excused myself from the class. I was so happy that I didn't have to go to school for three days. Pappamma had only been seventy-eight, but she looked very old. I always remembered her as sickly, but she was funny and very witty. She was very fond of my youngest brother, Ruki. She chewed betel leaves and sometimes had a cigar, too. She was lively.

I went to Dadda's sister's—Kamala Marmie's—house. A long, beautiful, black car followed his Morris Minor. "A. F. Raymonds" was written on the side of it. I decided that when I grew up, I would buy this car and take a lot of people in it. I noticed that at the back, you could actually sleep. That became my ambition—to own a car where people could sleep and travel.

The funeral was a very sad affair with a lot of crying and howling, although Dadda cried very little. That was him, but on the other hand, Mummy cried for everything. I stood outside the house and chatted to various people, young and old. I didn't know what to say. I made up stories about my Pappamma and told them. I told them how she did magic tricks for me, how she climbed the mountains in Hatton, how she played carom with us. I kept on creating stories. None of these old men knew who I was and had never met me before.

Pappamma was buried in Nallur cemetery. There was another round of crying before she was buried. After the funeral, we came back to Kamala Marmie's place. It was quiet initially, before some men arrived. They had gone somewhere from the cemetery and had some drinks before coming back. They slowly started singing old Tamil movie songs, and the place became lively. Three hours before, there had been a lot of crying—and now, a lot of jokes and singing. This is what happens when you die, I suppose. Life moves on and must go on. I lost both my grandmothers in two years and before I was eleven.

My parents left for Hatton, and we went back to our hostels.

Miss Thambiah informed me that I had won the fifth grade English Prize. Fifth grade prizes were always given out when you got to sixth grade. The prize-giving was held in the college grounds, and the chief guest was Rev. Peter Vaughn. His message was, "Leave the place better than you found it." I got a book by Enid Blyton as the prize: *The Mystery of the Invisible Thief*. That was the first storybook I ever got. I read about ten pages and fell asleep. I then couldn't remember what I read and would start reading all over again. I fell asleep by the tenth page. I never finished reading the book.

Only from sixth grade, hostellers were allowed to go for the "big match"—Jaffna Central versus St. John's cricket matches. This match was referred as the Battle of the North. Cricket was in the blood of all Sri Lankans, and there was no exception in Jaffna. Everyone played cricket. We always played this match at Central College grounds, as St. Johns had its grounds inside the college, and they feared crowd trouble and damage to the school. Everyone came for the match, including those who had nothing to do with the school.

We won the toss and elected to field. We lost the match by an innings. That was very sad. We had people crying, shouting abuse at the players, and blasting the coach and the college staff. There was a man who tied a knot around his neck and pretended to be dead, tied to a tree. We walked back to the college. Everyone was very quiet and upset. We went back to our hostels, took a shower, and then waited at the college grounds when the team arrived.

They came back by an Esty bus. We mobbed them, but they were in a very sombre mood. They had very little interest to talk to anyone but enjoyed the attention they got, even though they had lost by an innings. We all congregated in front of Memorial Block. We sang a lot of Sinhala *baila* and Tamil pop songs. Now everyone was laughing and became happy. I really enjoyed it, as I would do anything to avoid Studies.

I got promoted to Grade 7A under Mr. V. A. Stephen. He was our maths teacher. He was a very strict and serious man but also extremely kind and affectionate. He could be irritated very easily, and there was a particular sound—*dock*—that got him going. He couldn't handle that noise. When he heard it, he would get hold of someone randomly and thrash him. This became a good challenge for us. While we knew that he might thrash us if we "docked" him, we always hoped that he would pick someone else. Since he was a maths teacher, he also used his mathematical skills to calculate where the noise came from. He used some technique to identify the person, and no one ever worked out what it was.

We soon realized that he was vulnerable to a few other sounds, too, including *meow*. We had a small, round tin that made that sound when you turned it upside down. We had a plan to have this brought into the classroom and hid it inside the cupboard. We asked one of our naughty chaps, Nadana, to sit next to the cupboard and turn this tin every few minutes. Nadana agreed.

Ten minutes into our maths class, I signalled to him to turn the tin, and he obliged. "Meow…meow." The sound went on and on, and even when Nadana turned it back, it would not stop. Sir caught Nadana red-handed and asked him to come out of the desk and stand in a corner. He opened the cupboard and found the tin that was making the meow noise. He just took Nadana by the hand and started hitting him all over.

Nadana had a twin brother called Nadesa who had just had an operation in his stomach. But they were identical twins, and Nadana pretended that he was Nadesa and rolled on the ground, pretending to be hurt around the stomach area. Then he just stayed still on the ground, pretending to be unconscious. We knew he was acting, but he was not moving at all. Sir panicked.

"Kumaran, come here. He seems to be unconscious. He needs a hot drink. Here is one rupee. Go and get him a cup of coffee, very fast!"

Nadana, who was supposed to be unconscious, now opened his eyes slightly. "Sir, thank you. But instead of coffee, can I have Coca-Cola, Sir?" That was it—Stephen master was now furious. He knew that Nadana not only made the noises but had also pretended to be unconscious. He asked Kumaran to go back to his seat and severely punished Nadana.

Even though we made so much fun of Sir, he was a wonderful man. We owed our mathematics foundation to him. He taught us really well and made us understand the basics. He always gave us extra classes before an examination. He was so devoted and caring and wanted his students to do really well. When we moved on to eighth grade, we gave him a wristwatch as a present. We all collected money and bought it. We had a small social in our class, and Nadana presented the wristwatch to him. Sir got up to speak, but he couldn't do it. He had tears in his eyes and just smiled and sat down. He was one of a kind.

I continued my boarding life at Thompson when Thevathasan master married his girlfriend. This happened during our school holidays. It was a customary thing for the entire staff to felicitate the newlyweds. It was also customary for the couple to provide some short eats: mutton rolls, cutlets, and sandwiches.

Thevathasan master asked me to be in charge of the short eats that he ordered from the tuck shop. I collected the foodstuff and took it to our hostel. I went to have a shower. I came back to the hostel and found out that the boys had eaten all the sandwiches. They had very kindly left only the mutton rolls and cutlets. I had no choice but to take them to the function.

The couple was seated in the middle, and the staff around them. They were chatting a lot. Sir nodded at me to serve the short eats, and I did serve the mutton rolls and cutlets. He then nodded again, indicating to serve the sandwiches, but there were no sandwiches. I smiled back at him. He kept on nodding, and I kept on smiling. He couldn't say or shout anything from where he was seated. After we served tea, I quickly ran away from the staff room. He came looking for me, and I had no choice but to tell him the truth. He laughed it off. He was such a nice guy. He understood what went on at the hostel.

My promotion to Grade 8C coincided with me moving hostels. I was transferred to Dr. Rajasingham.

Evarts and Thompson hostels were the building blocks of my life at St. Johns. This was where the real foundation was built. We got used to living in an open dormitory, we got used to having toilets far away from where we slept, we got used to the different food, we got used to spending limited amounts of money at the tuck shop, we got used to playing various sports, and we got used to sticking to a strict routine.

The college bell, of course, kept us going, and it was a wonderful start to my college life at St. Johns.

The mail train slowly gathered speed and passed Navatkuli. This was where my uncle who had given me that white rope lived. I did remember seeing Navatkuli Station when we stopped to collect passengers. The next station was Chava, which was only three minutes away. Deva Uncle told me that he would go there with some food for me to eat on the train. He asked me what I would like, and I asked him to bring *pittu*, banana, and cuttlefish curry. I was to wave at him when the train got to Chava.

The train restarted from Navatkuli. I was determined to stay awake so that I could get my food parcel at Chava, knowing very well that I might doze off. I stood up and stretched my legs. Achchi kept looking at me. I asked her if she needed anything, but she just kept looking at me. I got a bit annoyed and sat in my seat. "If you are falling asleep, then that is fine, but please put your head on the other side—the window side, please."

I was a bit embarrassed and put my head against the window. The next thing I knew, the train was pulling away from Chava and picking up speed. I jumped up from my seat, put my head out, and shouted,

"Deva Uncle…Deva Uncle!" I saw him at a distance. He was very tall and bald. He was waving at me with the *pittu* parcel in his hand. He was getting smaller and smaller, and the train was going faster and faster. "Achchi, you got me to put my head against the window. Now see what has happened. I don't have anything to eat for dinner."

"You were asleep even before the train left Jaffna. What are you talking about? Are you at Jaffna Uni?"

"Why do you ask me that?"

"Oh, smart kids who study hard get tired, and they fall asleep at odd hours. I thought you were one of those super-smart kids."

"Yeah, studying is very hard. I study very late into the night. This trip is a good chance to catch up on my sleep. Unfortunately, it has cost me my *pittu* packet."

"Oh, *Thamby*, really sorry for you. Here, eat this. I got some rice and curry parcels. I brought two parcels—one to eat now and one to eat later, closer to Polgahawela. You can have one of the parcels. You are a kid who is growing up and studying hard. This country needs people like you." She was now affectionately calling me *thamby*: "little brother." She opened her rice packet and gave it to me. Achchi and her generation loved those who studied hard and went to university. They had a special place in society.

I was now taking advantage of Achchi. I did feel bad, but I was very hungry. I had a great dinner and asked her for some soft drinks. She opened a flask and poured a cup of coffee and gave it to me. "Thanks, Achchi. You are very kind. Any sugar?"

"No, *Thamby*, I am diabetic. I have to be careful. No sugar."

"What, no sugar? Who drinks coffee without sugar? Can you check in your handbag if you got at least one cube of sugar?"

"No. You should cut down on your sugar and be free of sugar."

I hated that cup of coffee, but I didn't throw it away. I struggled with it. It was the worst cup of coffee that I have ever drunk. "Goodnight, Achchi. You have been great. I better go back to sleep. I need to catch up on my sleep so that when I get to Colombo, I can keep on studying into the early hours of morning."

"Okay, *Thamby*. I will not disturb you. If you need coffee, please do ask me."

"Sure, I will."

She had no clue that I hated that cup of coffee. I turned my head and placed it on the window, and I saw Memorial Block.

THE MEMORIAL BLOCK

MEMORIAL BLOCK HAD FOUR HOSTELS: DR. RAJASINGHAM, HANDY, ALISON, AND CROSSETTE. I was now in Dr. Rajasingham. Our hostel was on the first floor, and next to ours was Handy, while Alison was directly below us with Crossette next to it. The toilets and the showers were behind this building, and some of the senior boys had the use of a well that was next to Crossette.

I did fare reasonably well at studies but did the bare minimum. My grades were good enough for me to achieve Good, and that took the pressure off me. There were some subjects that I was beginning to hate passionately—art, science, and history. My favourite subjects continued to be English, geography, and mathematics. I loved my sports and enjoyed playing the fool and irritating others.

My original nickname, Oothai Sinniah, matured to Sorri Sinniah. *Sorri* meant "pain" or "scratching." I was not sure why that was my nickname, but I know I used to always joke a lot and was a serious pain in the neck to most.

I continued to look for opportunities to avoid Studies. I took the opportunity to go and watch the Australian Under 19 cricket team who were to play the Northern Province schoolboys' team. It was wonderful to see foreign players, and this was the first time I had seen any. Northern Province lost by an innings.

Michael Lang was their star batsman and scored 157 runs. When he got his hundredth run, we all ran inside the ground to congratulate him. This irritated the Northern Province cricketers, including our own Thevapalan, who was the wicket keeper. He identified me and reported me to the principal. I was given a stern warning. He made me attend detention classes and got me to write, "I will never run into the grounds when the cricket match is on" one thousand times. I went for the match to avoid Studies but ended up getting detention!

"OC" was one of the most beautiful concepts ever developed in the hostels. It is a technique whereby you borrowed and wore someone else's clothes. Most of those who were not at my hostel never knew whose clothes I wore. Some had the impression that I had nice and clean clothes.

No one knew what *OC* stood for. They said it meant "on credit." Apparently, after the World War, the Americans gave Sri Lanka (Ceylon) flour and other goods on credit terms. They called this programme "OC"—"on credit." I was never sure of this story.

This was why my "Oothai Sinniah" nickname got upgraded: I took OC to the maximum. I never bothered whether I had good, clean clothes, as I was always confident that I could do an OC. This also helped me to dress well and properly for church. We continued to go to church three times every Sunday. The morning and evening services continued to be compulsory for all

Christians in the boarding school, and some of us had to attend Sunday school as well. Church was the only place we could see girls of our age, although it was difficult to talk to them. We could talk a little bit at our Sunday school classes, but it was still very limited.

At Sunday school, the girls always sat in front, and the boys sat at the back. The boys who sat just behind the girls had some chance. OC allowed me to establish some credibility with girls. Everyone in my hostel knew that I needed some quality clothes for Sunday services and Sunday school. I didn't even bother to ask them but just selected the best clothes of my friends and wore them. All the Christians in the hostel did OC. I always tried to select the clothes before they did.

Our hostel master, Mr. B. T. Jeyanandarajah, was an old Johnian and excelled in athletics. He was a no-nonsense man and very smartly dressed. He always wore spectacles, and that made him look very serious. Our hostel monitor was Frank Samuel. Getting into this senior boarding block was both exciting and scary, especially when you needed to walk downstairs in pitch dark to go to toilets in the night.

As thirteen-year-olds, we were now allowed to participate in college speech and poetry contests. I could speak decent English and was selected for it. All the contestants were asked to recite a poem called "Casabianca." (*The boy stood on the burning deck…*)

I put in a lot of effort and memorized the speech. There were twelve contestants, and our English teacher, Mr. S. K. Mahalingham, coached all of us. I was ready and excited about the contest. There were around one hundred students who had come to witness the competition.

My class had high expectations. Sri and I were their representatives. The judges sat in the middle of the hall, about fifty yards from the stage. Students from the other classes did their recitation. Sri gave a fantastic performance and received a loud applause.

It was my turn. I wore a white shirt, blue shorts, white socks, and black shoes, and all of them were OCed. I walked to the stage confidently, acknowledged my class, and stood proudly on the stage. The bell went, indicating that I got to start. I took two steps forward.

"Casabianca…errrrr…" I couldn't remember the second sentence. I coughed and started again. "Casabianca. Ummmmm…" Oh, no, I couldn't remember. I took two steps back, took a deep breath, and took a confident step forward. In a very firm voice, I shouted, "Casabianca!"

That was it. Nothing more came out of me. I kept looking everywhere except the audience, when the bell rang indicating that I had finished. I felt so miserable that I had not only let myself down but also let the whole class down. Sir told me that I had wasted an opportunity and should have given it to some other boy. "Oh God—one day, he will show mercy upon you and make you better." I walked slowly back to the hostel, took my clothes off, folded them nicely, and returned them to my OC supplier.

Our Tamil teacher, Mr. V. Subramaniam, tried hard. He was a simple man with simple clothes, dressed in *vesti* and always in white. He knew my Tamil was very bad and that I needed extra classes. He did that for no money. He was such a wonderful man, but he had a very short temper. This was something we were determined to test.

Grade 8C was next to the basketball courts. There we found a dead lizard. Sir's nickname was *Pambu*—that meant "snake." We devised a cunning plan.

In the front, right-hand corner of our classroom, there was always a wastepaper basket. We decided we would keep this lizard under the basket. We had a tall guy in class called Petman. His role was to go to the basket to put in some paper. While he did that, he was supposed to kick the basket by "mistake," exposing the dead lizard. When the dead lizard was exposed, Nadana, who was seated in the front row, would jump up and down and shout, "*Pambu, pambu, pambu!*" This would definitely irritate Sir, as he was fully aware of his nickname. It was a pretty simple operation. I was selected to give the signal to Petman once I got the signal from Nadana. We rehearsed it a few times before the Tamil class, and everything went off well.

Twenty minutes into the Tamil study period, Nadana turned towards me and winked. I looked at Petman and tapped three times with my pencil. Petman got up, took the paper, and walked slowly towards the basket. I could see Nadana getting excited and anxious. As Petman was getting very close to the basket, Sir walked to the front of the class and obstructed Nadana's view of it. Petman was still walking and was not even close to the basket, when suddenly Nadana shouted, "*Pambu, pambu, pambu!*"

Nadana thought Petman had moved the basket and exposed the lizard; he had taken a chance. But Petman was nowhere near the basket. Sir asked Petman to stand still. "Where is the *pambu*, *Thamby*?" He asked Nadana very politely.

"Sir, it is under the basket."

"How do you know? Even I can't see it from here. You must be a magician to see under the basket."

Sir then moved the basket, and the lizard was there. He knew this was a set-up. He called both boys to the front of the class and punished them. I escaped.

My grades continued to be reasonable, but I simply hated anything where I needed to read and learn. I was fine with anything with numbers or pictures, but even mathematics had a lot of theory. I would do anything to stay away from classes and Studies. We were attending art class when I heard that there was going to be a library reader's prize being awarded for the middle school. "There will be a test, and whoever gets the highest mark will get the prize. It is going to be held right now in the library," Sivamohan casually mentioned. I jumped at the idea and informed our art master, Mr. K. Veerasingham.

"You? Ha, ha. Library reader's prize? Go on—give it a try!" He laughed loudly.

I sat in the library for the exam. There were fifty questions, mostly on world affairs, and I answered them all. I won that prize with a score of only eighteen! The boys who came to do the exam were those who hated studies and would do anything to avoid classes. I knew the best students never sat for it. I never won any prizes after that.

I continued to play hockey under Thevathasan master for the third team. The boarders dominated hockey. My classmate Sivamohan was the captain. We had a lot of fun during the practice sessions in the evenings. I loved hockey and enjoyed playing in a team. We played three matches and won one and lost two. There weren't many schools that had third teams, and it was difficult to organize matches.

One of the highlights of the season was a match between Chundikuli Girls' College's first team and us. We rarely used any deodorant, and I wondered how the girls took to us, as we were sweating like pigs. They were all immaculately dressed. They came to play hockey, but they had lipstick on and tight, white shorts and T-shirts. I had the feeling the girls were not keen to play hockey but had come to impress the senior boys with their good looks, short shorts, and clean clothes. We wore white shorts and grey T-shirts made out of thick material that made us sweat more.

We lost the match four to two, but I scored a goal. While scoring the goal, I tripped and fell on top of the goalkeeper and seriously injured my ankle. She was big and tall and gave me one kick. I was so excited, as this was my first goal for college. It was an impressive goal, but sadly, the girls were all older than me. Normally, the girls eyed the boys who were around two or three years older than them. These were the ones we called *acca*, meaning "elder sister." You don't flirt with *accas*.

Basketball was becoming popular. Mr. Ponniah joined us as a boarding master and was in charge of Evarts hostel. He was also our basketball coach and was keen on starting a basketball team. I was keen to join and went for practice. I got selected for the third team. We played a few matches against YMCA and some combined teams, but never against other schools. I always came as a substitute, as I was not that tall. I found basketball a very good team sport. Sir was very strict and did a lot of warm-up exercises before practices that I hated. The court was tarred. We used to play without any shoes and in our bare feet. The court would get seriously heated. We would still play on with pain, as we had no other choice.

The boarding life was getting really enjoyable. Twice a term, we were allowed to go for a movie at a local cinema. We would normally be told on a Monday if the boarders would be going for a movie that Friday. It would cost us around one rupee and fifty cents.

One of those movies was *Vellikizhmai Viratham*. We were told that it was one of the best movies. It featured two of the best young stars: Sivakumar and Jayachithra. We assembled in front of the college hall and stood in two rows. The senior hostel monitor told us to walk, and we walked out of college, down Main Street, turned down Temple Road to Hospital Road, and came to Ranee Cinema. I saw on the top of Ranee a huge cutout of Sivakumar and Jayachithra. Sivakumar was holding her tight, and Jayachithra had a scary look on her face. I asked Thayalan whether it was a scary movie, and he told me that it was not. It was supposed to be funny.

When we went in, the crowd was shouting and whistling, and everyone was quite excited. Unfortunately, some of us did not get seats together and were scattered around. I sat next to a very old man, but I got an aisle seat. He had come to the movie with his daughter and her three small children. I had a chat with him, and he looked like a very religious guy. He had put a lot of holy ash on his forehead with a large, red *pottu*. I never knew men could wear *pottu*. He offered me a *vadai* to eat.

The cinema bell rang, and we all sat up. Sivakumar appeared, and there was a lot of clapping and whistling. He got married to Jayachithra. I thought this marriage happened too quickly. Normally in a Tamil movie, the hero goes after the heroine, who always rejects him first. He would try very hard and do some heroic stuff to win her heart. This cat-and-mouse game goes on till half-time. It was only during the second half that she would relent and marry him, but not before he has had a major fight with the villain.

It was a breeze for Sivakumar, and he married her within the opening few minutes. The movie looked a very serious one, and there was nothing funny. After they got married, they fell at their parents' feet, got their blessings, and went in a long Buick car for their honeymoon.

The car went down a main road and went over something. Sivakumar ignored it, but Jayachithra told him to stop. He said it was nothing and kept on driving. It was a snake that the car went over. At this point, I shouted, *"Aiyoo, amma!"* ("Oh, my mother!"), as I hated snakes.

I closed my eyes while the old man shouted, *"Arroharrah!"* (Something to the effect of "God is great!")

I continued to keep my eyes closed for a few more minutes. "Has the snake gone?"

"Oh, yes, God is great—the snake escaped."

I slowly opened my eyes as the couple checked into a hotel. They went into their room and sang a song—"Theviyin Thirumugham," a beautiful song that explained how beautiful the girl was and how smart the boy was. There was just one scene of the snake, and I was happy that the ordeal was over. The couple went to bed.

Suddenly, Jayachithra jumped up, woke Sivakumar, and pointed at the big chandelier on the ceiling. Sivakumar was annoyed and looked up. I had a heart attack. I screamed so loud and was short of breath. The old man kept on shouting, *"Arroharrah*—God is great!" There were about one hundred snakes on the chandelier. I closed my eyes and never opened them until half-time.

I went out and got hold of Thayalan. I was angry with him, as he had told me that it was a funny movie. He brushed me aside and told me that there were a lot of funny jokes.

"But there were snakes, *machchan*. I hate snakes, you know."

Thayalan looked very puzzled. "Oh, that, at the beginning. But after that, it was all fun."

I had missed everything. It seems there were no snakes after that chandelier scene. I had missed the first half of the movie, as I had my eyes closed. It made sense, as the old man never said, *"Arroharrah,"* after that. Half-time bell rang, and the movie started again.

The first scene was that stupid snake again. I shouted again, and the old man repeated his *"Arroharrah."* That was it. I closed my eyes and ears until the movie finished. I had no idea what the movie was about and what part the snake played. I didn't even know if Sivakumar continued to stay married to Jayachithra. One of the worst experiences of my life. I came out of the cinema and walked back with Thayalan. I slept so badly with a lot of snakes in my dreams, and I woke up screaming and scared.

Every hosteller was allowed to have two absits and two exeats per term. During absits, you could go out of the college for two hours but had to return by the deadline. Exeats were for weekends away. We went to 7, Dutch Road, Chava, for our exeats. My cousins were a lot younger than me, but it was always nice to see them. We would arrive on a Friday evening by Number 769 bus. Mary, their maid, would cook delicious meals, and we were always keen to have a good meal. After that, we would all sit in the hall and have a long chat and then go to bed.

On Saturday mornings, the three of us would go for a movie to Jaffna, and in the afternoons, we would join our cousins and play. We had to go to church on Sundays. My family belonged to the Anglican Church, but Aiyah was a key member of the local church, the Church of South India. After a good lunch, we would take the bus back to our hostels. Aiyah and Ranee Acca would give us two rupees each, and that would be very useful for us to buy extra food at the tuck shop.

Rajakulendran was one year senior to me and was a very funny guy. He and I decided to go to Jaffna town and have some *koththu roti*. We loved Mokkan Kadai, a great place to eat in town. We took an absit for two hours. We both had five rupees, and the bus tickets cost twenty cents each. We had our *koththu roti* and tea. It cost us two rupees each. We then walked towards Jaffna town and were going to take the bus back to college.

Rajakulendran saw a new ice cream parlour called Ricoh. Subhas Café was the only ice cream place for a long time. "*Machchan*, why don't we have some ice cream at this new place, Ricoh?"

"Great idea. Let us go in." We went in. We ordered a fruit-salad ice cream each. The waiter asked us if we wanted nuts on top. We agreed. He also suggested that we should have "double scoop." I didn't know what double scoop was.

"Do you want to mix and match?"

"What is that, *anna*?"

"Oh, you can have vanilla, strawberry, and chocolate."

"Let us have all three." I was keen to taste all of them.

"Yes, that can be done. But it will be slightly expensive." The waiter seemed happy.

"Never mind, we can handle it." I wanted it.

The bill came. We paid for it and had no money left for the bus. Rajakulendran was furious at me. He started shouting and blaming me, as we had to walk all the way back to college. We knew that if we walked, we would not be able to meet the absit deadline and would be punished.

We started walking fast down Clock Tower Road, past Jaffna Central College, and cut across First Cross Street to the main street. We were now running and came towards the water tank opposite Holy Family Convent when a car stopped by us. It was Mr. Anandarajan. He was our co–vice principal now. He offered both of us a lift and asked us to get onto the back seat.

We opened the back door and got in, but to our amusement, there were no seats. Rajakulendran looked at me, and I looked at him. It seems the car was given for service. The seats were always taken out before this old Hillman car was serviced. We had no choice but to stand at the back, and he took us to college. We had to bend a lot; that gave us a serious backache. All the excitement of the new Ricoh ice cream vanished fast. Rajakulendran was mad at me and told me that I had no limits and I didn't use my brains to think!

April Fool's Day each year was great. We all played some stupid practical jokes. We thought we would tie a cow to the college bell very early in the morning so that when the bell rang, all the boarders would get up, thinking it was five forty-five. Five of us woke up at four to get the cow. Tharmu, our key man, did not sleep at all. We caught the cow that was roaming outside the college. Benedict, our gatekeeper, was fast asleep, and the side gate was wide open.

We brought the cow in and tied it to the college bell. It started ringing very slowly: *ding*. There was a long pause, and then *dong*. Another long pause, and then *ding*. This went on for three minutes.

The stupid cow was so lazy and hardly moved. The bell did ring, but not with the usual frequency. It sounded more like our church bell. There was a practice in Jaffna that when someone died, the church bell would ring slowly, like what our cow was now doing. This made a lot of Christians around the school think that someone had died, and a few nosy ones now turned up at the church. The church keeper was asleep. They were getting worried and looked for the church keeper. We were hiding in the Williams Hall classroom, watching this.

The cow kept on ringing this bell slowly. We urged Tharmu to untie the fellow when the vicar appeared and called for the church keeper. He realized that the church bell was not ringing, but the college bell was. He walked towards our bell when Tharmu let the cow go. The cow ran towards the priest, and the priest ran inside the church. The cow didn't go through the side gate but turned back and ran inside the college grounds. All were running after the cow except me, as I ran back to the hostel and slept on my bed.

I understand Benedict caught the cow and got it out of the college. He was afraid that he might get into trouble for letting the cow in. None of the hostel boys woke up, as the bell didn't ring like the school bell. It was good fun but went badly. Tharmu came back to the hostel and slept as well.

Our Grade 8C (Form IIIC) was a great class. That year, we won the cricket matches against all other Grade 8 classes. We did well in football, too, but lost the finals to Grade 8D. Mahalingam master, our English teacher, ran two contests: the "Do You Know Contest" and "The Spelling Contest." We won both the competitions. We had a fantastic group of classmates.

This became very evident when our classmates Nadana and Nadesa's father died. We all went to the funeral, and we were all around them. They were crying, and we were consoling them both. I realized how close we were and how much we cared for each other.

History was the most boring subject. I hated it, and hated it with a passion. My ability to read and learn never improved, as I would attempt to read and ended up falling asleep.

Mr. A. P. P. Perimpanayagam was a very tall man and rarely spoke loudly but would quietly mumble through the history lesson. He gave us a lot of homework, and once he asked us to describe the fight between Ellalan and Dutugemunu. Apparently, these two kings fought a fierce battle in 161 BC. I had never studied this. I went to the class seriously underprepared and hoping that someone else would be called to describe it. Unfortunately for me, he picked me that day.

"Sinniah, I am sure you would have done your homework. Describe the tussle between these two great men."

I had no idea. I didn't even know that they had had a fight or for what purpose. "Sir," I started confidently, "fighting is not good. From small age, these two were told by their parents not to fight. You can see in the Bible, Sir. It is clearly quoted that no one should fight."

"Stop! Sinniah! Don't talk like a fool! They were not Christians. They may have been Buddhist or Hindus. Anyway, that is not the point. Get to the subject matter. Go on."

"Sir, when I think of these two, I think of MGR and Sivaji." MGR and Sivaji were two famous actors of Tamil cinema. They always fought, but not against each other.

"What?" he barked.

"Yes, Sir. Think about it. MGR is a fighter, but so is Sivaji. But very rarely, they fought together. I think, Sir, only in one movie,

Thundikulli, where they actually acted together, and I am not even sure they fought. Why, Sir, why? We should never allow these two great men to fight. Same thing here, Sir. Dutugemunu—and who is the other person, Sir? I just forgot—"

"Stop. You idiot. You have got no idea, and you are just talking all nonsense. You don't even know the names of the two people. Come up here."

He slapped me a few times and told me to stand outside the classroom. I did that until I saw our principal doing his morning rounds. He would know that I had disrupted the class if he saw me standing out. I would receive further punishment. I decided I would start walking towards the water tap. As I passed him, he greeted me. "Good morning, Sinniah. Where are you going?"

"Sir, a bit thirsty, not feeling well. Going to drink some water."

"Good. It is very hot today."

I went to the water tap, and I saw him talking to A. P. P. I walked slowly back to make sure that the principal was out of sight and stood outside of my class. A. P. P. called me in. "Yes, please come in. I understand you are not taking the hot weather very well today and a bit dehydrated. I am being informed by the principal, your honour."

I realized that the principal had told him to be careful with me, as I seemed to be suffering from dehydration. Next minute, I was on the ground, as A. P. P. had lost his temper and thrashed me. He was screaming and saying that I was behaving like a fool. I apologized, and that made him angrier. He calmed down and told me to sit down.

Kathir, our star student, was now explaining the fight. I was listening very carefully. Suddenly, A. P. P. stopped Kathir and pounced on me. This went on for about ten minutes. Despite all these incidents, I still loved him. He was a very humble person and very religious. He told me to take my studies seriously and not to joke around. We respected him a lot.

Our holidays in Hatton were great. Mummy informed us that my cousins Ravi and Usha were going to join us for Christmas. Ranjit Anna had already left school and was living in Colombo. My cousins were of similar age to Wijit Anna. They got together and started talking among themselves as soon as we got into the train. I could only hear names of boys and girls. I was thirteen, and they were sixteen. They were into boyfriends and girlfriends, and I could only sit there and listen.

At Chava, we got some food parcels from Deva Uncle. The train stopped at Kodigamam for fifteen minutes, and that allowed us to eat our dinner and wash our hands. I went to sleep and woke up at Polgahawela. Three hours later, we took the train, Poddi Menike, to Hatton. This train journey was so picturesque. We passed Rambukena, Peradeniya, Gampola, Nawalapitiya, and Ginigathena.

I always put my head out of the window and admired the landscape, especially the tea estates and the tea factories. We knew we were close to Hatton when we passed the tea estate Carolina, in Watawala. We would then see the beginning of Strathdon Tea Estate. We were just minutes away from Hatton. I was so excited, as I was going to see my parents and my two younger brothers. The train passed Hatton Rest House, the nursing home, and then Princess Cinema.

Dadda came with my younger brothers, Delano and Ruki. Mummy was at home, cooking our lunch. We had seven people in the small Morris Minor car. We went past Hatton and Dickoya Towns and turned right into Panmure Bungalow.

It was a beautiful bungalow that overlooked a small lake. We always had visitors. The bungalow had seven rooms. Another cousin of mine, Chooty, was also staying with us. In Dadda's family, there were three Chootys. His eldest brother's son, his younger brother's son, and me were all called by the same name. It was very confusing. My cousin Chooty was going to school, and we didn't get to spend much time with him during the day. He was there in the evenings.

December was normally very cold. We wore sweaters and had hot water to bathe in. During the day, the temperature rose to around twenty degrees. All of us—Wijit Anna, Ravi, Usha, and I—would go for long walks. We walked through tea estates and greeted local tea pluckers. We climbed rocks and crossed streams. It was great. We called it "The Walk." We wrote WRUC—Wijit, Ravi, Usha, and Chooty—on every rock we passed. We sat on the rocks and admired the scenery.

Once in a while, we would walk past a grave. In the tea estates, they buried the dead in the estate itself. The graves were just mounds of earth, each with flowers and a cross. Since Usha was a girl and I was small, Wijit Anna and Ravi would leave us close to the grave and run. They said that they could see ghosts and spirits. Usha and I would hang on to each other, shout, cry, and run behind them. They would go behind a tree and would shout and scare us when we ran past them. It was all good fun.

Dadda allowed us to go up the hills and run around the tea estate, but he always warned us to be careful and not to get lost. Four of us planned to go to the local *peeli*. This is where people went to have a bath in a local stream.

The group WRUC went off one morning. We took some sandwiches. It was a picnic. We went up the hill and started walking down towards the stream. We had to cross the stream to get to the *peeli*. There was a small plank of wood that was used as a bridge. Wijit Anna went first and then helped Ravi to cross. Usha, with her tight, red trousers, struggled to walk across, but both of them helped her.

When it was my turn, I was so scared and was shivering. It was a terrible ordeal to use the plank to cross the river. We marched towards the stream in the same order: WRUC. The three boys changed into shorts and went under the *peeli* and had a good bath. Usha, of course, stayed out, perhaps not wanting to upset her beautiful hair and her tight, red trousers! We had our sandwiches and started walking back. Neither Usha nor I realized that Wijit Anna and Ravi had planned to leave us alone and run away.

We came back to that small bridge. They went ahead, and before we could think, they both started running, leaving us on the other side of the bridge. We howled at them, but they ran away. We were again scared and started crying. Then we saw at a distance a road, but it was a significant climb. We couldn't cross the bridge without W's and R's help. We held each other and started climbing towards the road, still sobbing and crying. We saw a grave, and it seemed like someone had been buried only a few days ago. We were now screaming, scared of ghosts and spirits. We went close to the road and saw a lorry. The people in it recognized us and took us back to our bungalow.

By this time, Wijit Anna and Ravi had already gone home and told Dadda that we were coming in a lorry. It was a risky thing we had done. Dadda was very upset and flared up at us for coming in a lorry. We both cried again.

During the afternoons, we would play carom and Scrabble. As I was the youngest in the group, the others always cheated and made me lose. Our cousin Yohini Acca and her husband, Joy Anna, came to our place from Colombo. They bought from Cargills a board game called Multi Millionaire, a Sri Lankan version of Monopoly. I always came in last, as they would continually cheat to prevent me from winning anything. We had four table-tennis rackets and used the dining room table to play. We would line up a set of books as the net. We had so much fun. We would always go out for walks and played a lot of indoor games.

I came last in every game that I played with my group. Sometimes during the afternoons, the three others would go to sleep. This was my chance. I took my frustration out on my two younger brothers. I would summon them and tell them to be my students, and I, their teacher. I would use a stick as a cane. There were other students, too. These were all the plants that Mummy had nicely planted around our house. I had seven students—Delano, Ruki, and five plants. Two of the plants were rose bushes, and three were garden beauty.

The stage was set for the arithmetic class. I gave the students one simple task. "Multiply ten by three, and divide by six." I allowed them five minutes to answer while I went around them and the plants to make sure they didn't copy. Ruki had no idea. He was five years old, while Delano, who was nine, seemed confident. I didn't like that.

"I don't know. What are you talking about?" Ruki started to cry, and I gave him a few small taps with my cane on his palm.

"You get twenty marks, as you told me the truth. What about you, Delano?"

"Errr…thirty, and then I think it is five…the answer is five."

"What are you thinking? You are not sure? You took too much time. You get fifty marks, although the answer is correct."

I gave him a few taps, but harder ones, on his palm and on his backside. He started howling. I told him to cry quietly, but he wouldn't.

I asked the rose bushes and the garden beauty. I started really hammering all those five plants for failing the test badly. I hit them so hard that all the plants were damaged and broken.

Delano and Ruki ran inside crying and told Mummy. She came running out to find me hitting the plants very hard. Mummy then took the stick from me and started hitting me. That was the end of my arithmetic lessons for my two younger brothers and those five plants.

Two days later, around ten o'clock in the morning, there was some shouting around the lake. People were running up and down, and our maid, Mary, told us that someone called Gangamma had committed suicide by jumping into the lake. WRUC went into operation and decided to go there. The crowd was held back as the woman's body was recovered and laid on the ground. She was bloated, and her face looked disfigured. WR immediately went on to second gear. They told UC that her ghost would not go away from this lake and would visit it and nearby places tonight. I dismissed this immediately but was worried.

That night I had a dream. Gangamma came and asked for me. She knocked on the door and asked me to go out. She was upset that I went to see her that morning and said that I was laughing a lot. She said that I insulted her and that she was going to take me and dump me in the lake. At this point I woke up and cried loudly. Dadda and Mummy rushed into our room. They scolded me for going to see Gangamma and took me to their room. I slept in their bed.

During the April holidays, we always went to Nuwara Eliya. It was the best season to be in the hill country. We would leave Dickoya very early in the morning and reach there around ten. We would drive straight to watch the Magastota Hill Climb. This was the annual motorcar and motorcycle races. We would park the car where we could conveniently have our food and watch the races.

Bri Ponnampalam, Priya Munasinghe, Mana Jayawardena, and J. P. Obeyasekera were in their prime, and it was great to watch them. When we came back home, we would select one of these drivers and run around the house like them. My favourite was Priya Munasinghe, who drove a Mini Cooper. I was determined to buy a Mini one day.

After the races, we visited either Nuwara Eliya Gardens or Hugalle Gardens and enjoyed having ice cream and iced milk from Milk Board. We would end the day by going to see Mummy's cousin Hari Uncle. We loved our trips to Nuwara Eliya. My parents had apparently lived there when I was a baby.

We would spend most of the time at home and going for walks. For WRUC, it was almost a daily routine to go for walks and end up with fights between WR and UC. WRU were old enough to join the choir of our local church, Christ Church, Dickoya. They were being trained for our annual Christmas carol service. Mummy was the organist, and Mr. Jeyasingh David was the choirmaster. We always had nine lessons and nine carols. I was to read the second lesson. It was a pretty drawn-out service, and most of the English songs I didn't even understand. The fun part happened after the carol service as thirty of us joined the carol singing.

The carol singing started around nine in the evening. We would get into a lorry that had no chairs, so we sat on the floor. We then went to Christian homes to sing carols and wish them well for Christmas. My aim was slightly different. I couldn't sing, so my sole focus was to eat and drink as much as I could at these homes. We would go to the Abrahamses', Edward Raj's, the Packianathans', the Devans', and finally, we ended up at the Williamses' house, where a thumping breakfast would be served.

By the time I got to the Williamses' house, I might have eaten ten Christmas cakes, twenty mutton rolls, ten cutlets, and another ten patties. I would have drunk about ten glasses of soft drink but just a cup of coffee at the Williamses'. We would wear sweaters and thick trousers. We had a marvellous time and really enjoyed the night out. Dadda picked us up in the morning. Christmas was very enjoyable. The carol service was always held on the twenty-third, and we wanted ours to be better than the one at the Methodist church.

New Year's Eves were spent at church. After the service, we would go home to have a big breakfast; it would be *kiribath* with sugar and banana. Dadda gave us each a one-rupee coin. This was called *kaivilayam*—for good luck. You are not supposed to spend that one rupee until the next year. I always kept it with me throughout the year.

My parents took us, including Ravi and Usha, to Colombo. We stayed with Dadda's sister, Baby Marmie. She was very fond of us, and her daughter, Loga Acca, was our chief guardian. Loga Acca would take us to the zoo and to the SSC swimming pool. She bought us hot dogs and ice coffee from Fountain Café and got us nice chocolate slabs from Zellers. She always looked after us and treated us very well. She kept us very busy. She took us to various English movies, even though I had no idea what those movies were about.

One of the movies was *Patton*. The main actor was George C. Scott. I knew I was scared of snakes, but this guy kept on shooting everyone and everything in sight, including a camel and a horse that I couldn't work out why. Loga Acca always bought an Elephant House Ice-Choc during the interval. Sometimes I slept through the whole movie. The whole experience in Colombo was great, and I got to know a different part of Sri Lanka.

We left by Yarl Devi from Colombo Fort to Jaffna. Delano was joining us at the boarding. I felt really bad for this small, tiny guy when Dadda and Mummy kissed him good-bye. We all got food parcels from Baby Marmie. She made scrambled eggs and roast beef sandwiches. I was keen to attack the food parcel as soon as we left Colombo and asked for my lunch parcel from Wijit Anna.

"It is six thirty in the morning. You just had your breakfast at home, and now you want your lunch?"

"That is fine. Give me my lunch parcel."

"Real *madayan*, Mariamma."

That made me cry. Mariamma was my nickname, and as soon as they mentioned it, I would cry or lash out at them. My family created a story that I had been adopted and that my birth mother's name was Mariamma. Apparently, she had left me in a drain because I was ugly and naughty, and my new parents felt so sorry for me and took me home.

Dadda had enough of this and had banned that name in our house. When he was not present, everyone else would all say it, and I would react badly. Later on, my brothers used any name starting with *M* and told me that it signified Mariamma. I started to react badly to *any* words starting with M. Dadda then banned any words starting with M!

While I had a superb time in Hatton during the Xmas holidays, I was looking forward to being back at boarding. I was really enjoying my hostel life at St. John's. I was getting to like the food. I enjoyed playing sports, although I was not good at anything in particular. My grades continued to be all right, and I managed to pass most of the subjects. I really treasured the friendships being formed at school and in the boarding. We were all very close. No one could touch a boarder, as we were there for each other, and unconditionally. We thrived on practical jokes and banter.

"Barrrrley…barrrley…barrrrrley…" I knew we were at a station—Anuradhapura, the old capital of Sri Lanka. I was pretty annoyed at being woken up by this idiot who was selling drinks. I had only one rupee in my pocket, and I looked at Achchi.

"What, are you going to buy barley?"

"Love to, but I think I left my money back at uni."

"Really, you should be careful, *Thamby*. There are all kinds of people in the uni, and they can steal your money. Smart boys like you must be careful."

"Yes, I need to be careful."

I laughed inside myself. This poor old lady believed that I was at uni. There was zero chance of me ever going to a university, and I was fooling her. I felt bad about it, but what could I do? I needed food and now barley.

Achchi bought me barley. She asked me to buy from the vendor, as I was seated next to the window. I bought two barley bottles and gave her one.

I needed to go to the toilet. I jumped over Achchi and went there. When I came back, Achchi had moved to the window seat and was looking outside. It was very dark, around two in the morning. There was nothing much for Achchi to see.

I glanced to the other side of the compartment. Sitting diagonally opposite of me were two nuns. One nun looked older but not as old as Achchi, while the other looked very young. The younger nun's uniform came up to her ankle level, and I could see her ankles. She had beautiful ankles. I had never focused on ankles. This was new and exciting for me. Her head was covered, and she was looking out the window. I was desperate to see her face. "Hello! Can I borrow your paper?" I shouted across. The young nun was reading *Ceylon Daily News*.

"Here, you can have this," the older nun replied, giving me her paper.

"But I want hers."

"Why? It is the same newspaper."

"Really?"

"Here, take it." She forced it on me.

The younger nun didn't even bother to look at me, but she was laughing. She knew that I wanted to make some connection. I kept on looking at her ankles. They were great, but I needed to see her face.

We came to Kurunagela. I couldn't believe that I had been awake since Anuradhapura. That must have been a record for me.

The train reversed from the station and was held back, as there was another train coming from the opposite direction.

There was only one track, and the trains stopped at stations to allow oncoming trains to pass. This was a great opportunity for me. I went to the nun's window and poked my face out. Although the train came from my left side, I kept looking at the right, as I wanted to see her face.

"Child, the train is coming from the left side. See, see? Other side," the old nun advised me.

"*Thamby, kavanam, thallaiyai kondu poga porthu!*" Now Achchi was shouting and warning me to be careful, otherwise my head might roll away. "He is a lovely boy and is at the uni. Looks very smart. He studies very long hours and sleeps very little. He was catching up on his sleep in the train. Parents may not be giving him enough money. He had no food and no money for barley," I overheard Achchi telling the old nun as they started a conversation.

"Why don't you go and sit next to Achchi?" I advised the old nun.

"Thank you. And you can sit here." I got to sit next to the young nun now.

"What is your name?" I asked.

She turned towards me with a smile. She was biting her upper lip. She had one of the most beautiful faces ever. I never realized you could read faces from the ankles. "Sister Mary. You?"

"Sinniah...I am at Jaffna Uni."

"Really? What are you doing?"

"Engineering. First year."

"Oh, good on you. Christian?"

"Oh, yes, Anglican."

"Have you joined the Uni Student Christian Movement?"

"Yes, I am very active."

"Funny, as I am the advisor to SCM, and I have never seen you there."

Jesus! I was being caught here. I tried to change the topic to distract her. "Is it raining outside? Look, be careful. You better close the window; otherwise, you will get wet."

"How can you see the rain? It is so dark out there. Anyway, this Jaffna Uni…"

"Oh, I need to go to the toilet. I'll be back soon. Barley is creating trouble."

I ran to the toilet and waited there for a few minutes. I looked at her from afar. She was stunning. This could be my chance. Could I ever convince a nun to give up her faith and marry me? Perhaps it was too much to aspire to.

I came back to the seat and didn't want to disturb her. I just kept looking at her ankles. I wanted to marry her, but I had some doubt that she would if she actually knew that I was not at uni. She opened a small box of Kandos chocolates. She passed it on to the older nun, who offered some to me. I turned and looked at my darling nun, who smiled and said, "Eat."

Oh, yeah, she must be keen. Why would she smile? Why would she ask me to eat? But why didn't she offer me the chocolates directly? Maybe to hurt me. They say the person who hurts you most is the person who loves you most. I was now completely convinced.

This was it. I was going to ask her directly about our marriage, and I was planning my attack when my eyelids felt heavy once more and started to close. I tried my best to keep my eyes open, but as usual, I couldn't. As I was dozing off, she opened an envelope and took a piece of paper out. It looked like a prayer, but it was a letter.

I started to dream. I dreamt that letter. I was opening that envelope.

Our family in 1969 after my cousin Yohini Acca and Joy Anna's wedding. I am standing next to Mummy.

Some of us in front of the college gate. Sivaguru always stood here and sold ice cream to all of us.

HOCKEY — 1st XI - 1977

Standing (L to R)   N. R. Lewis, U. X. Pushparajah, B. S. Sinniah, A. Muralitharan, G. D. Anandarajan, S. J. Jebaratnam, V. Thavathurai, S. Jeyakumar, A. Kannapiran.

Seated (L to R)   Mr. N. S. Thanapalan (Coach) K. Kumarakulasingam (V. Capt.) The Principal, A. Sripathy (Capt.) Mr. J. N. Ponniah (Prefect of Games)

Ground (L to R)   S. Srijeyan T. Kanthasamythurai.

THE PREFECT BODY

Seated (L to R)   A. K. Sivasothy, L. D. Mahendra, S. Uthayakumar, G. D. Anandarajan *(Dep. Senior Prefect)* J. R. Joshua, *(Senior Prefect)*, S. Kadirgamanathan, S. J. Jebaratnam, J. R Coomarasamy, P. Shantbakumar, The Principal

Standing 1st Row (L to R)   N. R. Somasundaram, A. Sripathy, J. Jebaratnam, N. Sivasumathan, B. N. Sinniah, N. Shanmugaraiah, T. Anpalakan, N. Kathiresan, M. A. Benjamin, K. Tharmalingam, E. Eugene kulasingam, N. Yogarajhen

COLLEGE ATHLETIC TEAM - 1977

Ground (L to R) P. Sutharsan, S. Srithayalan, S. Sriganadas, S. Suresh, T. Arthithan, S. Varathan, S. Kulendran.
Seated (L to R) Mr. K. S. E. Xavier (Coach), K. Kumarakulasingam, P. T. Rasiah (Captain), The Principal, A. Muraleetharan, (Vice Capt.), N. Varnapahan, Mr. J. N. Ponniah (Prefect of Games)
Standing 1st Row (L to R) N. R. Somasundaram, S. Sritharan, K. Jeyaram, K. Jeyakanthan, T. Aspalagan, S. Shanmugarajah, S. Thananjeyan, S. Parthipan, B. S. Sinniah, S. Sivasutthiran, M. Gobalan,
K. Velesan, P. Shanthakumar
Standing 2nd Row (L to R)

The suitcase that I won with Mummy's help
from the Young Timers Club.

JAFFNA BOY

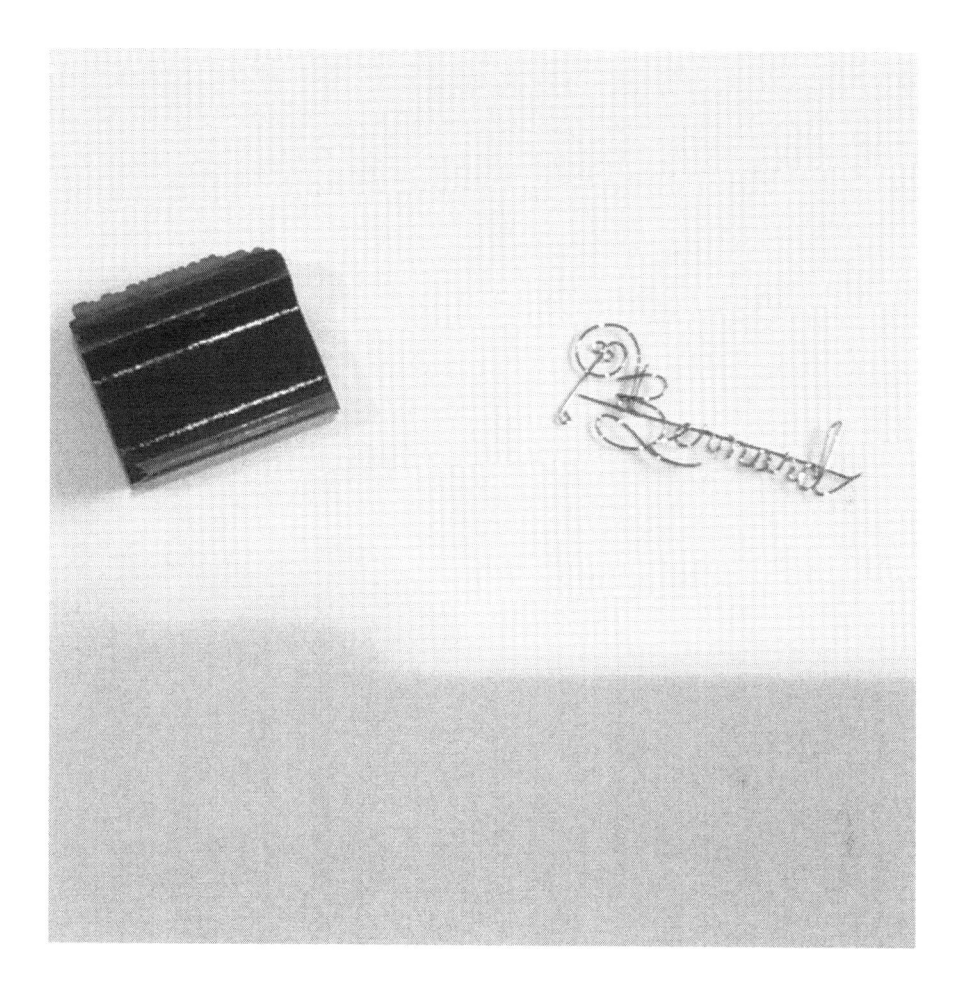

The presents I got from my pen friends.

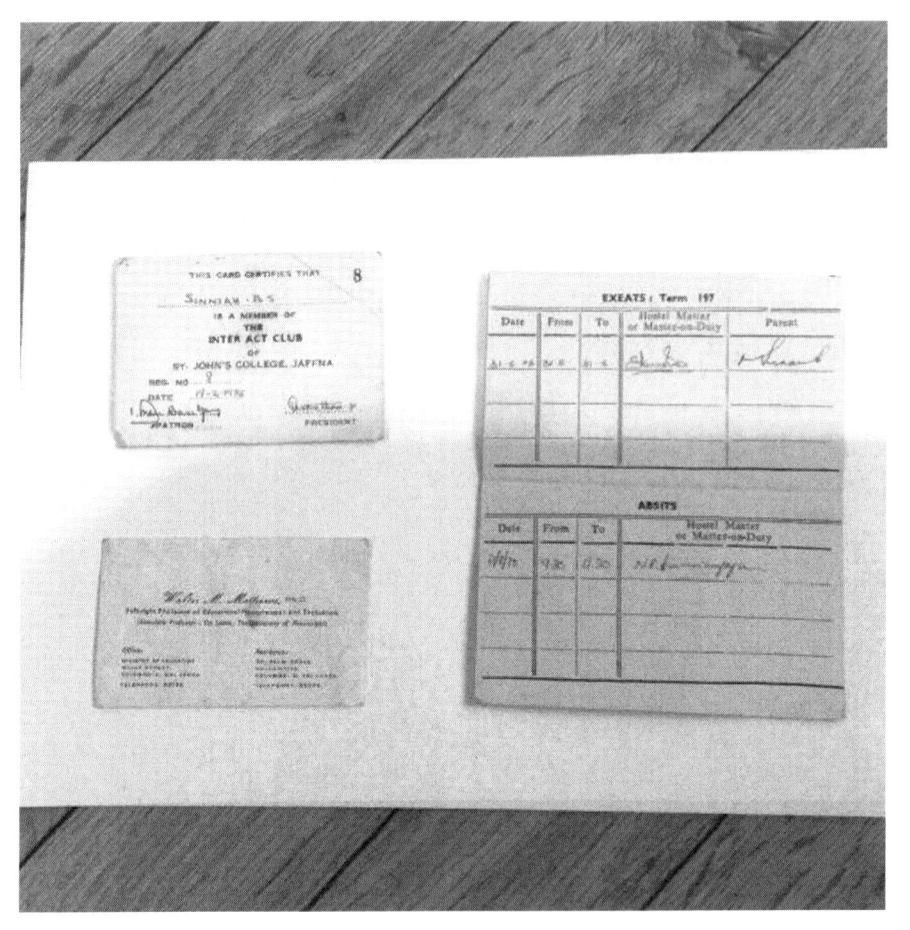

Membership card of Interact Club, a visiting card of the Fulbright professor, and an exeats/absits card. You can see Dadda's signature and Mr. N. R. Arumainayagam's signature.

My dear Sujatha: *Annakilli* movie songbook
and a movie ticket from Lido Cinema.

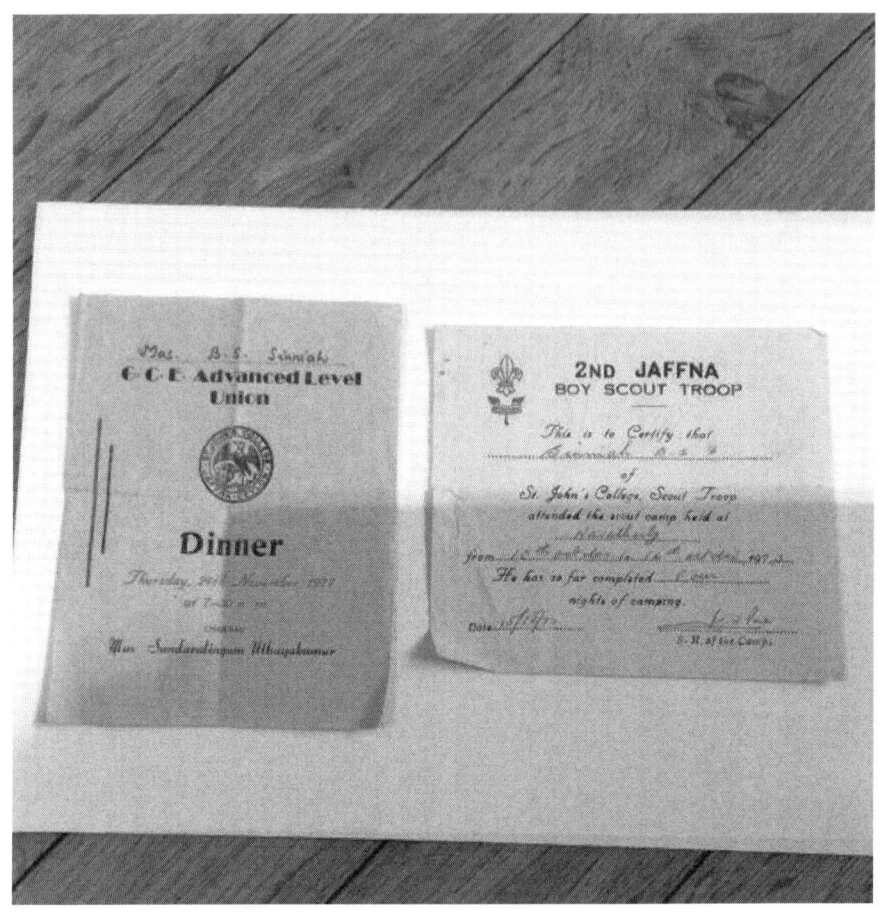

A-level dinner invitation, 1977 and my scout certificate

My instrument box and my KG pen.

In front of Memorial Block:
Vijayaparathy, Frankie Samuel, Gopinath, Nirmalan, Thigamparanathan, Sivagnanasegaram, Muralitharan, Lingathas, Wijit Anna, Kumarakulasingham (KK), Premnath.

Seated: Sathanathan, Sivasothy, Thevathasan, Sivarasa, Tharmakumar, me, Surendra, Yogalingham, Saseetharan and Ravindran.

Interact Club, 1977

Lower VI social invitation and my college prefect badge.

JAFFNA BOY

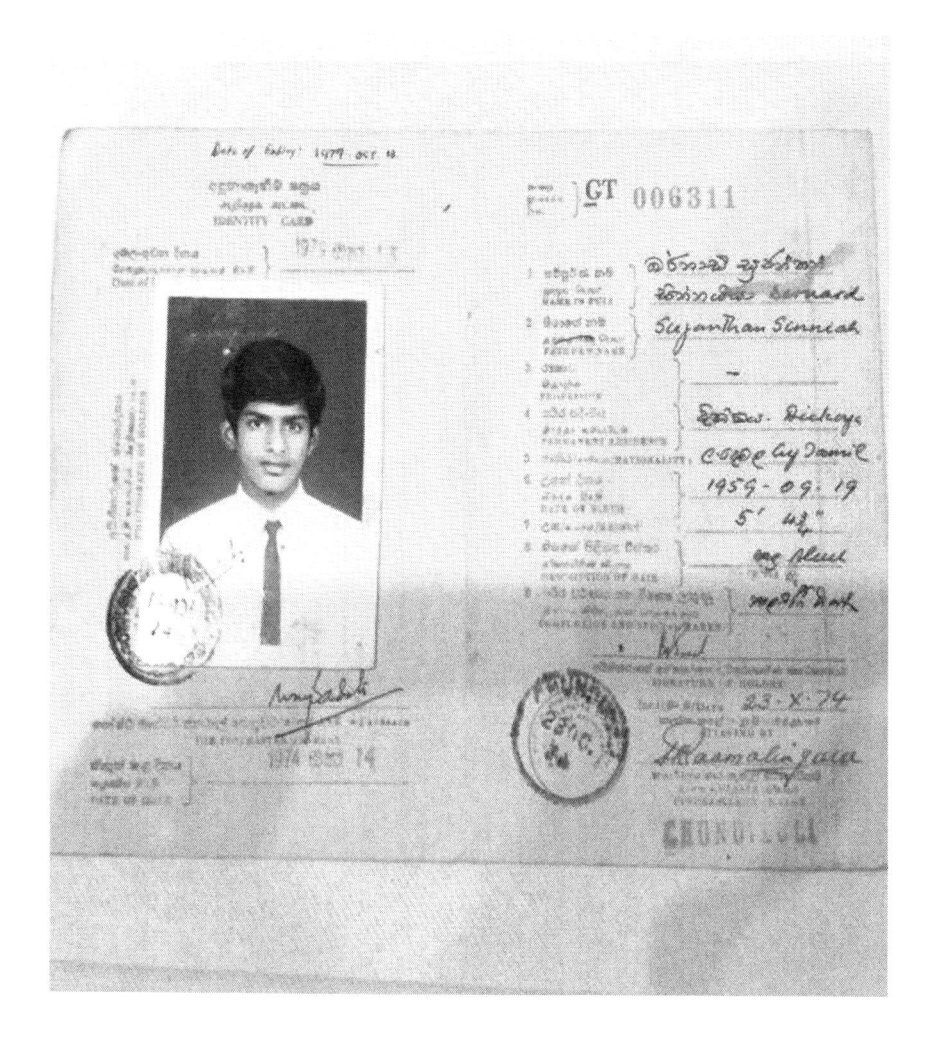

EDWIN J. JEYARAJAH

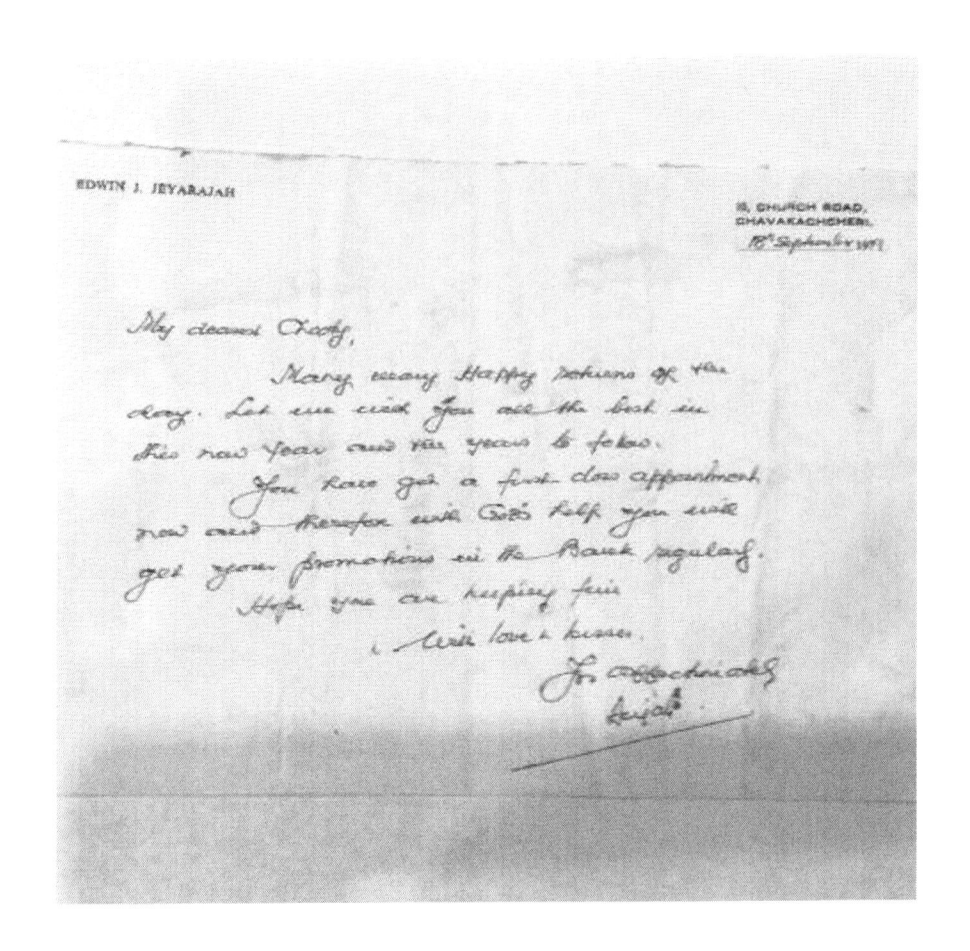

15, CHURCH ROAD,
CHAVAKACHCHERI.
15th September 1971

My dearest Chooty,

Many many Happy returns of the day. Let me wish you all the best in this new year and the years to follow.

You have got a first class appointment now and therefore with God's help you will get your promotions in the Bank regularly.

Hope you are keeping fine.

With love & kisses,

Yours affectionately,
Appah.

Thirty-five years later, Gnanaponrajah (currently the principal of St. John's College) and me enjoying the dining room bell.

THE RISE AND FALL OF SOMASUNDARAM AVENUE

WIJIT ANNA CAME LOOKING FOR ME AT LUNCHTIME. I was joking around as Ramu was distributing *porricha meen* (dry fish). I was tickling him under his belly button. He took a swipe at me when Wijit Anna appeared. "Hey, Chooty. Great news. Read."

"What?"

"Yes, great news. I will talk to you later." He gave me an envelope that was already open. Mummy had beautiful handwriting, and the envelope was addressed to him. I opened the letter. I didn't smile for a few days!

It read:

My Darling sons Wijit, Chooty, and Delano,

How are you all? By God's grace we are all fine here in Dickoya. Dadda is busy with his inquiries and I am busy selecting the carols for our Xmas service. We are looking forward to seeing you all soon.

I wanted to share some good news with you. Dadda and I have decided that it is best for us to rent a house closer to St. John's so that all of you can live with me. Ruki can start his schooling at Chundikuli Girls' College next year. Dadda will of course stay here in Dickoya and will continue to work. He will visit us every month, and we can come back to Dickoya for our holidays. This is very exciting news, and I wanted to share with you all immediately. I have never had you with me during the school days, and it is great that we can all live together...

"What?" I screamed. "No, no, no. This cannot be true. Happy for us? Noooooo! You cannot think like that!"

I was now very upset. I was not happy at all. This was not exciting. I loved the hostel life, I loved my friends, and I loved the fun. I was going to give up all that—for what? On top of that, there would be pressure to study. It wouldn't be regimented, but the nagging from Mummy to study would be high. I couldn't do this, but I had no choice. The decision had been made.

Mummy and our maid, Mary, joined us after Xmas holidays, and we rented a place closer to St. John's at 28, Somasundaram Avenue. I simply hated it. I missed my hostel mates and the fun. The food was, of course, so much better, and my brothers were happy to be with Mummy. But not I.

Ruki joined the nursery at Chundikuli. I had to take Ruki to school to drop him in front of the Chundikuli gate. I then walked to my school that was just two minutes away. This was not as bad as I first feared, as there were a lot of girls standing in front of the girls' college.

Somasundaram Avenue was a beautiful street with nice houses, and most of them who lived there knew Mummy. One of my closest friends, Sethu, was living next to us. Two of my classmates, Sriharan and Jeyaram, lived opposite to us, and we walked to school together. Two other classmates, Angelo and Kathir, who lived a bit closer to college, always joined us.

Wijit Anna was a top class sportsman at college and was good at any sport he played. He was a great cricketer, played hockey brilliantly, and was a superb footballer. He was also great at table tennis and carom. To top it all, he was very handsome, well dressed, and walked with some grace. This went down beautifully with girls, and all admired him.

Then you got me! I tried playing sports, was decent at hockey, a shocking fielder at cricket, and scared of the ball in football. I hated snakes and dressed poorly. I never cared about dressing up, rarely wore shoes and always wore slippers. Whenever the strap of the slippers broke, I used a safety pin to pin it to the base. I wouldn't even care if the slippers were of different colours. I never combed my hair. However, it never stopped me from dreaming that some girl, someday, would fall for me!

The Under 14 cricket team was formed, and I went for practices. We had a trial match. I was in a team that had Fowzan as captain and Mahendra as vice captain. Shanthy was in our team. We fielded first. The opposition had great players like Ratnarajah, Nanthy, Big Jeba, Kutty Jeba, and Mootai Murali. Sethu was their off spinner. I am not sure on what basis they took me into the team, but I was still considered to be a good left-arm leg spinner.

The openers walked in, and I was at short leg. First ball was quite high, and the batsman fended it off. It came straight at me. I closed my eyes, and the ball fell on top of my head. Dropped catch. I was immediately moved from there to mid-on. Next over, Big Jeba flicked the ball down the leg side. It caught the outside edge of the bat and flew straight at me.

Why? What?

Yes, the ball was coming towards me. I waited, staggered a bit, and ran towards the ball. It fell three yards away, on my left side. I misjudged its direction. I was moved again, but this time to fine leg. I was happy to be fielding there, as no one scored there.

We were doing well and had them down at eighty runs for six wickets. There was then a partnership between Nanthy and Ratnarajah. Nanthy was smacking us all over the place. They put on fifty runs, and this was getting out of hand.

They never hit one ball to fine leg. I would field at fine leg, and for the next over, I would cross the entire ground to field at fine leg on the other side. There was zero confidence in my fielding ability. I had bowled two decent overs and given away thirteen runs, but once Nanthy came to the crease, I was taken off.

I was getting bored, so I kept chatting to the crowd. Shanthy came to bowl. I was fielding closer to the college tank and wanted to drink water. There was a tap next to the tank. Those two had now put on eighty runs. I waited till Shanthy finished bowling his third ball of the over, ran to the tap, and started drinking. Shanthy took a shorter run-up and bowled the fourth ball that was hit straight up in the air towards fine leg. Every fielder shouted, "Catch it, Sinniah!"

I was still at the tap and ran towards the ball. I stumbled on the boundary rope and fell flat. The ball fell close to me and passed me to go over the boundary line. That was it, and everyone was annoyed. Mr. J. R. Gnanapragasam, our coach, was livid.

Nanthy got out in the next over, and the innings folded quickly for 175 runs. I was relieved, but no one said anything.

It was now our turn to bat. M. Y. A. Fowzan and L. D. Mahendra opened the batting and put on 160 runs. I went in next with fifteen runs to get. I walked, took my guard, and surveyed the field. I had seen Gary Sobers in a film that they showed at College Hall. He had counted the number of fielders before batting. I did the same. Someone behind the wickets shouted, "He is the worst fielder in this world, and he thinks he can bat. I know what he gets for arithmetic. This fellow can't count!"

Umpire said, "Left arm over."

Within a few seconds, my wickets were on the ground. I did not see the ball. Ratnarajah bowled at a lightning speed. By the time I took my bat forward, the fielders were rejoicing my wickets. That's how fast it was bowled. That was the end of my trials. I became the scorer of the team and had a chance to go for all the matches—meaning not going to school. That was a great alternative.

I had joined the Boy Scouts movement so that I could avoid Studies and school. Ponniah master was in charge, while Thevathasan master supported him. The camps were held at Keerimallai, Kayts, and Ilavalai. Thevathasan master's relatives gave us a piece of bare land in Ilavalai to hold our camp. We were divided into four teams. We put up four tents to sleep in and dug some holes as toilets. In the middle of the camp, we had a special tent for the kitchen. A few boys were tasked with cooking dinner, and I was part of the group that was asked to prepare a short drama for the entertainment at night.

We woke up at seven. We were severely bitten by mosquitoes during the night. We sang our college song and saluted as the college and 2nd Jaffna flags went up. Ponniah master wanted to know if we knew how to swim. Four of us couldn't swim. We were told to stay back to cook lunch while others went for a swim. Thevathasan master was staying back to supervise. He went to meet his relatives and left us alone to cook the lunch. The swimmers were expected later in the afternoon.

Raj, the oldest of the four nonswimmers, suggested that we should test the local tavern and drink toddy. I wasn't keen. He assured me that toddy would be good for me and clean my stomach of all bugs. He was seventeen, I was fourteen, and I listened. The other two, Anandan and Preethi, didn't object, and we went out. Raj advised us to smoke when we drank. He bought cigarettes and two glasses of toddy. I took my first cigarette pull and almost died coughing. Raj advised me to take it in slowly. Preethi was an expert in cigarettes, while Anandan refused to smoke.

We smoked and drank toddy. I was getting very happy, and everything seemed great. The sun was shining directly on my head. I became happier and happier, and the sun was going up and up. I then began to go down and down, towards the road. I fell flat on the road and felt something happening in my stomach. The hot sun was doing some mysterious stuff to my stomach, and I got up to stand again. I fell. I got up. I fell again. Raj came and asked Preethi to hold me. They pulled me up and dragged me along the road. We did make it to the camp. I saw Thevathasan master, who looked angry. "Where did you all go?"

"Sir, Sinniah was missing. We went in search of him."

"What? Where did this fellow go?"

"Tavern, Sir."

I could hear, but I couldn't talk. "Howowooeoeo, Sir… thessssssse booooooyyyyyyyys…" I said, and I fell flat on my face and started vomiting.

Sir had always been fond of me. He took me to the toilet and gave me a good wash. He took the hose pipe and watered me down. I changed my clothes and slept inside my tent. I was feeling a lot better. Ponniah master and the swimmers returned. The food was ready. Sir and others had done a great job. Ponniah master was told that I was having a bad stomach. "Oh, really? Poor chap. Kanthan, get an egg coffee for Sinniah."

Oh, brilliant. Egg coffee! This is special. No one gets egg coffee at a scout camp, I thought. I got my egg coffee and had a lovely sleep. I joined the other scouts only for dinner and slept again.

I got promoted to Form IVD. This was the class for the best students; I had somehow gotten into it. Our class teacher had been Mr. Sigmaringham, who unfortunately died of electrocution at the Tamil Conference. Mr. V. R. Amarasingham became our class teacher.

In Form IV, we had only eight subjects: English, Tamil, pure mathematics, applied mathematics, chemistry, physics, biology, and Christianity. Biology was by far my weakest subject. We had to get through our GCE ordinary-level examinations next year. We needed to have four credits and two passes at a minimum to pass O-level exams. This was two years ahead, but I had already decided which subjects I would focus on. I decided on English, Christianity, physics, and pure mathematics.

I hated studies, but so far I had survived, and I was now part of the best class. My problem had nothing to do with how my brain functioned but that I fell asleep every time I read more than two paragraphs. I simply could not focus and do any studies. Even if I had tried, I would not have gotten biology. It was a shocking subject, and I couldn't understand anything about plants or the human body. Amarasingham master's son, Amaranath, was a very close friend of mine. We were in the same class.

Sir gave us a biology test. It had only five questions that attracted twenty marks each. I had no idea how to answer. I took a chance. I answered all the questions with the same answer. I was hoping that Sir would not notice it. Sir started distributing the test results. I got my answer paper, and I got twenty-two marks. This was bad, but at least not zero. Amaranath, who was seated next to me, got eighty-eight. I assumed that was the highest mark for the class.

"Students, I gave you the exam yesterday, and I have given your marks today. That's how fast, like a computer, I have corrected your answers."

I could never wait without interrupting. "It looks like the computer can easily identify his son," I joked to those around me, but unfortunately, Sir heard it.

"What? What did you say, Sinniah?"

"No, Sir, it was a joke."

"Oh, really, it was a joke? Very funny. Can you repeat it?"

"Ehhhh…Sir, it was just a joke."

"No, I tell you to repeat it."

I did. He asked me to come in front of the class. He was a short man, and I was fairly tall. He found that he wouldn't be able to hit me due to the height difference. He asked me to kneel down. He then took his wristwatch off his hands, placed it on the table, and looked at me. His mouth was shivering with anger. He thrashed me really badly. I was on the ground. I could have gotten up, but I gave him respect and stayed on the floor. He paused. He then pounced on me. He paused and pounced. This went on for some time.

Sir was furious that I had accused him of being biased towards his son. Actually, there were about ten others who got more marks than his son. I knew Sir would never favour his son. I was wrong to joke, but I had to make fun. That was my duty. He became very fond of me, though, but gave up on trying to teach me biology!

A pretty, thin lady came to take our English lesson. Her name was Chithra Rajadurai. She taught us Christianity, too. I was reasonably good at both of these subjects. I engaged in them very actively with the added encouragement of having Miss as our teacher. Everyone agreed that she was pretty and that she used nice perfume. We did not use deodorant, but we all liked to be close to her just to smell that perfume. She wore a *mookuthi* (nose stud). She was a wonderful teacher, too. She really worked hard to teach us.

We finished reading *Coral Island*, and she wanted us to write an essay about it. I did read the book, but I can't remember any of the facts. We heard that Miss had a boyfriend called Nalliah. I took the opportunity to write an essay to expose this. I wrote:

> *Once upon a time, there was an island called Coral Island. A ship got wrecked close to the island. Nalliah was the captain of the ship. Chithra, a beautiful girl from the island, found him unconscious. She gave him fish and some loaves of bread (taken from her Christianity class). She fell in love with him. Nalliah was not that keen, but Chithra was begging him to marry her. She sounded quite desperate…*

Miss was furious. She called me and Nanthakumar, who came from Chava, to come up. He had copied my essay, word for word. "What were your thoughts when writing this garbage? Tell me."

Nanthakumar looked at me and then looked at her. He said he had copied me. I now needed to give Miss a quick explanation. "Miss, *Coral Island* is too much of a westernized story. I thought I would make it more local. See, Miss, this will be easy to read and understand."

"Oh, really. Where did you find these names?"

"I just picked these names, Miss. Do you like it?"

At this point, she became very quiet, and I thought she looked very calm. She called the class monitor, Aso, to come in front to keep the class quiet. She walked out of the class. Everyone was happy, as there would be no English class today. Some of the studious ones were upset with me, as I had upset her. Everyone liked her.

She returned after ten minutes. "Sinniah and Nanthakumar—go to Principal's office." She had gone to see the principal. I had crossed the line. I felt bad for Nanthakumar, but it was his fault for copying me.

We went to our principal's office. Mr. Nadarajah wanted to know why we were there. I told him that the principal was very happy with our studies and wanted to chat with us. Twenty minutes later, after getting six strokes from our principal's cane, we left the office. Mr. Nadarajah asked us whether the principal had caned us because of our superior performance and then laughed loudly.

We settled down at Somasundaram Avenue, but this new life was not something I enjoyed. I really didn't like this arrangement at all. The toilet in this house was outside, and my mother always locked the doors. I had to wake her up if I wanted to go to the toilet, and it annoyed her. She gave me a chamber pot and told me to use it and clean it up the next day. I really hated this life.

The food distribution in Jaffna was getting difficult under Srimavo's government, and you had to queue up to buy everything. Wijit Anna was our family hero, and heroes shouldn't be sent to buy bread. It became my duty to stand in the long queues to buy bread.

Sethu, too, had similar duties. We used to go to Piggotts, a shop close by, to buy bread and eggs and walk back cursing that we had to do all these little duties. I was really annoyed, as I never did any of this stuff at the boarding. It was a painful routine. But there were some benefits to this.

On Saturdays, both of us would go to Sinnakaddai, a market closer to Jaffna Town, and buy meat. We normally left around nine in the morning, took a bus from Kachcheri, and returned by eleven. It would give us enough time to go to school to watch a cricket match or play inside our own compound in the afternoons.

Bulto was getting very popular in Jaffna. It was a beautiful toffee. We could buy two Bulto for five cents. Sethu and I decided that we would take the bus one way and come back walking. This way, we could save fifteen cents—that could buy a lot of Bulto. This seemed an excellent idea, and we executed it perfectly.

We bought the meat and a lot of Bulto. We walked back, happily eating. We passed Jaffna Convent and crossed the railway line when it started to rain. We ran and stood under a tree. It did not stop for a long time. We were soaked to the skin and walked back slowly to our homes. I can't remember what had happened to Sethu, but Mummy expected me to get back by eleven so that she could cook the meat for lunch. She had invited some people over for it. About this, I had not been informed.

I opened the gate and walked slowly towards the front door when Mary came running out. "Where were you, *Thamby*? All the visitors are here, and we haven't cooked any meat yet."

"What is the hurry? Cook now."

"Cook now? It is two o'clock."

"Really? Oh God, I didn't know that we were this late. It rained."

Mummy saw me and smiled at me but continued to talk to the visitors. I went inside and changed into dry clothes and joined my brothers, who were all playing outside. "Mummy is very angry. You will be punished after the visitors leave," Wijit Anna declared proudly.

Mutton curry was cooked fast, and lunch was served by three o'clock. The visitors ate and left immediately. They didn't even wait for desserts to be served or have a cup of tea. Mummy waved them good-bye and immediately turned towards me. "You are a fool. You are so irresponsible. Where were you? I am going to punish you for coming back so late. I don't know what you are doing. Your grades are poor, and you don't study at all."

"Oh, really? What did I do? It was raining."

"What? You would normally be back by eleven. Even with the rain, at least you should have been here by noon."

"I didn't know you had visitors. Why didn't you tell me that in the first place? We decided to walk back."

"You walked back from the market? Why?"

"Bulto."

"What—Bulto?"

"Bought Bulto and ate it."

"So?"

"So we had to walk. We used the bus ticket money."

"Oh God. Why are you torturing me? You are so difficult, and I don't know what to do with you."

I was now getting used to Bulto. I was addicted to it. As a Bulto addict, I started using the ten cents I was given to donate to the church collection to buy them. Now I needed something to put into the church collection bag. I started using bottle tops, as they made the same sound as coins. I was good at it. I would put my hand right into the bag and just drop them. While this made the correct noise, no one knew what or how much I was donating.

Mummy decided to send me for tuitions. She sent me to Mrs. Nathaniel, who lived a few houses away from us. But my grades didn't improve. Mummy then arranged classes with Miss Chelliah. She was my friend Vijit's eldest sister. She, too, lived down the same road, but nothing seemed to work, and my mother was fed up. "I sent you to the left. It didn't work, and I sent you to the right—that, too, is hopeless! Where do I send you now?" Mummy was referring to the two classes that I had attended down the road.

My friendship with Sethu was getting stronger and stronger. He was a lot shorter and smaller than me. We went to school together and would walk back home for lunch together. We would do this every day. I would leave home and go to his gate, where he would join me. We walked up Somasundaram Avenue, passed the cooperative store, walked down Kandy Road, and turned into Old Park Road at the corner of the Acca and Sons shop. We then walked down Old Park Road and entered the college through the gate next to Selverajah master's house.

The Old Park Road walk was becoming exciting for us. Most of the girls who went to Chundikuli passed by Old Park Road. Some of them rode bicycles, while others walked on the left-hand side of the road. The boys walked on the right-hand side. There were some really good-looking girls, and some chatted to the boys, but not with us. There were a few letters exchanged, but sadly, nothing came to me.

The interaction with girls went up a notch when we started going for our confirmation classes. Our priest, Rev. A. J. C. Selvaratnam, was a jovial person and an old Johnian. He was married into the famous Handy family, who had close connections with our school. Confirmation classes took place every Sunday morning at the Figg Hall. We went home to eat our breakfast after the services and came back for these classes.

There were no tests at the end of the confirmation classes, and I liked that. You got confirmed automatically, and after that, you could receive bread and wine—the Holy Communion. Siva, who was not a Christian, told me that I could drink unlimited wine after being confirmed. This was one benefit, and the other was the opportunity to meet and talk to girls. Even in a spiritual setting, the girls were attracted to the same type of boys—the ones who were good-looking, great at studies, excelled in sports, and were well versed in the Bible.

At the end of each class, Rev. A. J. C. would ask us if we had any questions. Once all the questions were answered, we would be allowed to go home. These classes took at least an hour—sometimes two hours. They became quite boring and put me to sleep even though they were held in the mornings.

I decided that I needed to somehow impress the girls. I needed to do something that would not only impress them but also make them want me. We were discussing the Ten Commandments, and I made my move during the question time. "Pothakar, how do you get paid?" We called our pastors *Pothakar*.

"Why? What has that got to do with the Ten Commandments?"

"Just want to know. Am I right in thinking that your job is to preach on Sundays, do these confirmation classes, and then do the evening service?"

"Yes, that is right. But we are expected to do more during the weekdays."

"But then the sixth commandment says, 'Thou shall keep the Sabbath day free.' Not to work on Sabbath day. But you seem to work on Sabbath day. Aren't you committing a sin?"

His face turned red. There were some laughs on the boys' side, but none of the girls found it funny. "Sinniah, first of all, you can't even recall the number correctly. It is the fourth and not the sixth commandment. I need to meet your mother. I have got serious concerns about you. I am not sure if we can confirm you."

The class ended, and one of the girls confronted me. "That was a disgrace. Disrespecting our *pothakar*. We feel that you are a stirrer and we should avoid you. Perhaps you have got demons inside you. You need to confess to Pothakar and clean yourself up."

That was a serious nail in my coffin. I said sorry to Pothakar. "Okay, Sinniah. Too many jokes, and too many distractions. I am glad you came to apologize. I will forgive you, but I need you to behave and concentrate."

I was so happy to get out of this mess. Mummy would have blown her top off if she were summoned to meet Pothakar. She was already annoyed with all my antics.

The college sports meet was held on a Saturday. I went to the grounds on Friday and helped our Johnstone House boys put up the house tent. It was nicely decorated. We borrowed blue sarees to decorate the tent, as our house colour was blue. Handy House had the best tent. Their colour was green, and they could use leaves and plants to decorate it—and those were freely available.

I participated in the long jump and was knocked out during the first round. I was determined to participate at the sports meet. Senior sports meet attracted Chundikuli girls. The first round and the heats were held during the week, and only the finals were held on a Saturday. There were no events left that would allow me to shine and impress the girls.

"*Machchan*, have you thought about the obstacle race?"

"What is that, Sethu? Obstacle to what?"

"*Machchan*, you want to impress the girls, right? Most of the athletes will not participate in the obstacle race. This is your opportunity, man. Go and impress."

"But is it on the main day?"

"Yes, of course. I might think about participating, as well."

This was great. I spoke to our captain, who was pleased. He wanted two participants for Johnstone and was happy that I volunteered. "What is an obstacle race?" I asked him.

"Don't worry. But please bring two bananas, a bottle of cream soda, a saree, a blouse, and a wig."

"What? I thought this was a race."

"You will learn more on Saturday. Just come with these things."

I was ready on Saturday, but not before I had a bit of a drama with my mother. I approached her in the morning of the sports meet. "Mummy, they have selected me for the obstacle race."

"Oh, yeah. Well done. Something is better than nothing, I suppose."

"No, no. It is a prestigious race. Only a few people are selected. Sethu told me."

"Okay, if you say so." She looked at Wijit Anna, and both giggled.

"They need two bananas, a bottle of cream soda, a saree, a blouse, and a wig."

"Ask Mary to get you all that."

"I need a blue saree, as I am representing Johnstone House. Blue is our colour."

"You don't need to have a blue saree. Any colour will do."

Wijit Anna got involved. I told him to mind his own business. I wanted to do it in style.

"I don't have any blue saree," Mummy said. "The only blue saree I got is the one I wear for weddings."

"So?"

"So, I can't give you that. You will spoil it."

"No, I need a blue saree." I started to howl and cry. This tactic had been going on for some time. Every time my mother disagreed with me, I would howl and cry and make a drama. She would then give in.

"I am not giving you the blue saree. Get something similar to blue." She gave me a purple one.

"You don't treat me like your child. I never get what I want. Wijit Anna gets everything."

I walked past Wijit Anna and gave him a kick. He kicked me back, and we both rolled on the ground and had a good fight.

With my two bananas, a bottle of cream soda, a purple saree, the blouse, and the wig, I marched to the sports meet. The obstacle race happened after all the track events finished but before the final event, the fifteen-hundred-metre race.

I went to the starting point. It was a one-hundred-fifty-metre race, and at every fifteen metres, we were required to do something. They were referred to as obstacles; hence the name "obstacle race." At the first obstacle, you needed to wear the saree with the blouse and the wig, and at the next, you had to drink the bottle of cream soda. The third was where you needed to eat the bananas with other fruits that were provided, and finally, run to the finish line.

The Johnstone House captain cautioned me about the seriousness of the race. We were ranked fourth and only three points ahead of Peto House. His instructions were to finish the race but not to come last. It seemed an easy task.

The starter blew the whistle; I ran fast to the first obstacle, dressed up fast, and took off from there. I was coming in second. I ran towards the cream soda bottle and gulped it so fast that I had to burp pretty hard. I slowed down a bit, as I couldn't breathe properly. I went to the bananas station. I loved bananas. I wanted to eat them slowly and nicely, and I did that.

I looked up to see that almost everyone was on to the final station except one. He was just in front of me. I took off and ran towards the obstacle, which was a plate of fruits. There were local Thollakatti grapes, a mango, and a small apple. I had eaten mangos before, but grapes and apples were new to me. I ate them very slowly and truly enjoyed them. I had completely forgotten that I was in a race. I came in last, and the captain refused to talk to me.

Wijit Anna said that I had spoilt for Johnstone House, and it was a disgrace to the Sinniah family. I just kept quiet and mumbled that I had gotten carried away by the beautiful fruits. We did finish last!

I went home and was very disappointed with myself. Mummy was talking to my other brothers when I walked in with the bag with the saree and the empty bottle. "A true hero! What a disgrace. Everyone at the sports meet was talking about you. I overheard someone saying that Visaran"—madman—"Sinniah lost it for Johnstone house. What were you thinking? Don't I feed you at home? You ate as if you had never seen food in your life. Look at Sethu. He finished way before you. That is being responsible."

She gave me a knock on my head and asked me to wash up and get ready for dinner. Mummy was seriously challenged with my behaviour and found it difficult to handle me. I hated this life, as I wanted to be back at the hostel with my mates.

Everything came to a head one day. Sethu and I caught up as the lunch break bell rang, and we were walking back home. Panchayan, a classmate of ours, was trying to annoy Sethu. I wasn't sure what the history was between these two, but he was trying to push Sethu towards the Old Park Road wall. Sethu was trying to push him back but couldn't. He warned Panchayan, "Look, I got Sinniah, and if he gets angry, then he will smash you."

I was very scared of this guy, but I couldn't let Sethu down. I took a stick with thorns. I warned him to stop. He didn't. Then I started to whack him with this stick. He was bruised and bleeding badly. I dropped the stick and started running, and Sethu followed me.

Panchayan was on the ground, crying and bleeding. We both went home and had lunch. We went back to school. Panchayan approached us and told us that his parents would talk to our parents. He had a lot of bandages around his legs and hands.

After school, we went back. We played one-bounce catch in the front yard. Wijit Anna was batting. We had no bats. The bat was made from coconut tree. Mummy walked in. She was walking very fast and looked furious. She passed us and stood at the steps. She shouted at me. "I just came back from the Principal's office! What did you do to that boy? You hit him so badly, and he had been bleeding. Why are you doing this to me?"

She started crying. Wijit Anna asked Mummy what had happened and hit me with the bat. I ran out of the gate onto the main road. I started shouting, "Someone, please help me. My family is trying to kill me. Please help me, *now*!"

A guy on a bicycle came towards me, held me by my hands, and inquired about the incident. He was very drunk and was unable to hold on to the bicycle. He let go of the bicycle and went inside our house. "Why are you killing this innocent boy? You should be ashamed." He demanded an explanation while holding on to the doorframe. He could hardly stand. He was reeking of toddy and *beedi*, a local cigarette. He was burping a lot, too. I thought he was going to throw up!

Mummy told him to go away, and he just left like a mouse and didn't put up any counterargument. I was disappointed with him, as he didn't plead my case strongly. She was now crying uncontrollably.

I felt bad. I went close to her and wanted to kiss her. I wanted to say sorry, but she didn't want to talk. She got up and went inside her room. I felt very anxious, but she came back with a pen and a piece of paper. She started to write a letter. The letter was addressed to my dad. She asked him to give the house back and put us all back in the hostel, as she was sick and tired of handling me.

Two weeks later, I went home for lunch. We were all seated and eating when Mummy said that she was moving back, and we were all going back to the hostel. I tried to keep a straight face, hiding my excitement, but Wijit Anna was so angry and upset. He blamed me for this. I smiled and kicked him under the table.

I got up and washed my hands. I went into the toilet and let out one hell of a sigh of relief.

"Oh, yeeeeeeaaaaaaaah."

"What? *Thamby*, wake up. You are shouting and nodding off on my shoulders. I had an operation only recently."

Achchi was pushing me aside, and I was holding her tight and still shouting. She kept pushing me aside. I immediately looked for Sister Mary, but she was not there. "Where are they?"

"Who?"

"The nuns."

"Why?"

"Just looking for some spiritual guidance and wanted to have a chat after my sleep. Have we passed Polgahawela?"

"You are such a great, God-fearing kid. Yes, they got down there and are on their way to Peradeniya."

"Oh, really, that is my fate?"

"But the little sister left a short note for you. Here it is."

Oh, yes. I knew it. I knew that I could get her to be attracted to me. She was going to be my life partner. I was sure she would marry me. I was ecstatic, and I opened the envelope.

Thamby. Read Leviticus 19:11: "Do not steal, Do not lie; Do not deceive one another." The old lady was very kind to you and gave you food and drink. You deceived her by saying you are from Jaffna Uni but I know you are not. Hope you will change for the better. God bless you.

Sister Mary

The world came crashing down. She had called me *thamby*, which meant she was older than me. No girl married a younger man in Jaffna, and so marriage was ruled out. She also knew that I had been lying to Achchi. That was the end of any hopes of marrying Sister Mary.

I was depressed and fell asleep again. Achchi was pushing me aside. There were not many people in the compartment. I went to the next seat. I borrowed her pillow, stretched out, and fell into a deep sleep.

THE RETURN

I WALKED BACK INTO MEMORIAL BLOCK. This time, I was welcomed back into Handy Hostel. Karthigesu, Gnanaponrajah, Alphonsus, and M. S. Chinniah were there to greet me and welcome me. I was back at home once more.

Handy Hostel had all my old friends, and it was very easy to settle in. Mr. S. Mahendran was our hostel master. He was very handsome. We teased him about all the good-looking lady teachers. Whenever a good-looking teacher joined our college, we would speculate whether she could capture the heart of our master. He was a very soft-spoken and kind-hearted person and a great physics and mathematics teacher.

I was so happy to be back with my old friends. I soon realized that we had to attend a third Studies. When I left, we had had to attend only two Studies. But once you got into Form IV, you were required to attend the third, too. It was only for forty minutes and finished by ten twenty, but it felt like two hours. Whatever little interest I had in studying completely vanished. We could attend

Third Studies wearing our sarongs, and this made most of us fall asleep.

I continued to play hockey and played now for the second team. Alphonsus, Sivamohan, and I were selected to represent Jaffna District Under 15 Team. I was really thrilled. We had practices at Jaffna College and played a few matches before we went to Colombo to participate in the All Island Tournament that was held at Health Grounds, Borella.

We had a very decent team, but we came against a strong Colombo Blues. We got thrashed six to nothing. All three of us played, but for the second match, they dropped me. I played right half, but a good attacking player from Mahajana was brought in. The match was against Uva Province, and we narrowly beat them two to one. Our second goal came at the last minute. We played our last group match against Colombo Reds, and I played in that. I was fortunate to score a goal, but we lost four to one and were knocked out of the competition. We actually played really well compared to other districts, but we were bunched with very strong Colombo teams.

Alphonsus took me to see his mother. I had never travelled in Colombo alone without my family. We went to Wellawatte and to his house, a beautiful old mansion at 83, Hampden Lane. His mother was living there with his grandmother.

We had lovely food, and it was a welcome relief. The food at YMCA, where we were staying, was very basic. We had a shower and changed into our clean clothes. Aunty gave us some money. We walked down to Galle Road, took a bus, and got down at Cream House in Colpetty. Alphonsus knew all these places. We had ice-cream *faluda* and then took another bus to Colombo

Fort. By the time we returned to YMCA, the team had arrived back. We all had a good chat, and our coach, Mr. Anantharajah from Jaffna College, spoke to us. He told us that we should be proud of ourselves and that everyone had been complimenting us. We lost, but we gave our best and played really well and respected referees' decisions without any protest. He then asked all of us to stand up and clap our hands together in appreciation of each other.

This is the first time I came to meet students of similar age from different schools. The team went out to Majestic Restaurant and had *koththu roti*. We returned by Yarl Devi train to Jaffna. It was an awesome experience. While we didn't win, I formed great friendships with wonderful people from Jaffna College, Jaffna Central, Jaffna Hindu, Mahajana, and Stanley.

All newcomers to the hostel were asked to take the stage at the first Saturday literary meeting. As I had just returned to Memorial Block, I fell into the same category.

Newcomers could be asked to do anything, and it was called ragging. I was a champion at it and had ragged most who were now in the audience. It was their turn to do it to me. I knew that I was going to be a target. They all shouted my name. It seemed to be a unanimous decision to rag me first. I pretended not to hear my name when Sugumar walked up to me and pulled me forward. The president called for questions from the audience. "Ask Sinniah anything. But do it in an orderly fashion. No shouting. One by one."

"But President, really! They can only ask me to do one thing? One thing only?"

"Ha, ha, ha!" A lot of laughter from the audience. "This is our turn," everyone joined. The president didn't overrule them, as he, too, had been a victim of my ragging when he joined the hostel.

They asked me to do several small things, and then someone from the crowd shouted, "Tell us the alphabet backwards!"

"Z-Y-X-W-V-U…ummmmmh…ummmmh…"

"Oh, oh, oh! You failed. Let us give him one more."

"Can you swim, Sinniah?"

"No, I can't."

"Really? Let us see if you can." They brought a bucket of water. They poured the water on the ground, and it created a small puddle. "Okay, Sinniah, imagine that as a swimming pool. Now try and swim."

"Oh, it is hard."

"Come on. Get on with it."

I knelt down, fell into the puddle, and started flapping my hands and legs, pretending to swim. They were cheering me on as if I was at an Olympic event. My shirt and part of my trousers were getting wet. The president, A. S. Thayalan, got up from his chair, shook my hands, and welcomed me back to the hostel.

We were getting along as a close unit and were told that the annual Boarders' Day would be held soon. Karthigesu was looking at various Tamil plays and was deciding on one. Mahendran master walked by and overheard us. He asked us which play we would be putting up, and Karthigesu told him that we planned to do a serious play. He smiled at us. "Serious drama with Sinniah and Chinniah? You got to be joking."

"Why, Sir?"

"Listen…play to your strengths. You guys have a lot of funny and idiotic people here. Why not do a comedy drama?"

"Sir, then we need to write it."

"Do it. Nothing is easy."

It was a simple conversation, but with a great lesson from a great man: "Play to your strengths, and nothing is easy." He gave us so much encouragement.

We sat down with him and thought it through. We created a comedy drama: *Dr. N. O. Know*. Sir was the brains behind it. He wanted to create a nutty doctor who met different patients, diagnosed weird ailments, prescribed unorthodox medicines, and did crazy surgeries. He selected me to play the doctor, the lead actor. I had come a long way from holding that fan and the wooden pole when I was at Evarts.

We entered this drama for the Boarders' Day. Some of the other dramas were funny, but we were very confident. We practiced a lot in Sir's room and were well prepared. We wanted to get at least the third prize.

The bell rang. Sir sat in the audience and looked nervous. He had always been a tower of strength. I looked at him and entered the clinic. I had a nurse, and Gnanaponrajah played that role. He was already in the clinic and greeted me. He summoned the first patient, and it was M. S. Chinniah. I asked his mother, "What seems to be the problem?"

"He fell off the tree and seems to be unconscious."

"Now, what tree did he fall from?" There was a shelf of books on stage, and I picked a book about trees. "At what degree to the ground did he fall?" Then I took a mathematics book. I asked all kinds of stupid questions and then came to the last book. "I am so sorry, but according to this book, he is dead." At which point, M. S. got up and walked out of the clinic. We heard a loud applause from the crowd, which was going wild with laughter. It encouraged me. I got more confident.

We had a few patients coming in, including Rajkumar with a bent hip. Dr. N. O. Know took an iron from the cupboard and ironed him straight.

Last, Karthigesu came in, saying that he had eaten a lot of fruits and had a stomach ache. I touched his stomach, and it made some noises. I inquired whether he had eaten carrots and perhaps some jackfruit. He said he had. I asked my nurse to get the operating theatre ready.

There was a bed and a white screen, which was made out of a white linen bedsheet. All the lights were turned off, and I started on the operation behind the screen. We had torches behind the screen to create shadows; the audience saw only them against the white screen.

I started the surgery. I took a huge butcher's knife and pretended to cut up the patient's stomach. I took out bananas, brinjals, carrots, and finally, a huge jackfruit. I was, of course, taking them out from under the bed, but the audience only saw the shadows of the fruits. It looked as if I was taking them out of his stomach. It made everyone laugh, and with that, I said I had had enough for the day and walked out. That was the end of the performance.

We had superb reviews by the main judge, Mylvaganam master. The other judges were Miss Thambirajah and Mr. Kathirgamathamby. They praised us and said it was a hilarious drama.

We won the first prize. We were thrilled. We started hugging each other while Sir was calmly seated in the crowd. The judges then announced the Best Actor's Prize: Dr. N. O. Know! It was an amazing feeling to beat so many great actors. I felt very proud and wished my parents were there to watch me receive the award.

We were all so happy and were very grateful to Mr. Mahendran. Thevathasan master, who by then had left the hostel, helped us with the lighting for the final "surgery." He was so humble and helped us a lot even though he was a teacher at college. Mahendran master left us soon to join a private firm—Mercantile Credit. We owed a lot to him.

The fancy-dress competition was held in the evening and in the college grounds. The team discussed it and agreed that I would go as a statue. I was dressed up like a scarecrow and walked towards the area that was set up for the contest.

I stood there without moving for three minutes. I saw an ant very close to my right foot. It started to climb up my legs and was trying to get under my trousers. I didn't know what to do. I bent my knee and moved my leg up. Some people in the crowd noticed and started clapping. The ant continued to climb up and neared my sensitive areas. I brought my hand down and tried to push it away. At this point, the crowd was laughing and clapping. Even the judges were pointing at me and saying something to each other. They were all of the opinion that my movements were part of the act. They had no idea of the ant inside my pants!

I realized that my movements were entertaining the audience and then kept raising my legs and moving my hands, while the ant was very happy with whatever it was biting. The crowd loved it, and I couldn't believe it, although I was in severe pain. I did win the first prize. The judges said that it was a unique idea—a moving statue. I won the Best Actor and the Fancy Dress Prizes but had serious ant bites.

While I enjoyed the return to boarding life, Third Studies were a nightmare. I continually fell asleep and always got pulled up by the hostel monitors. They would ask me to go out and wash my face and come back to study. I would fall asleep again, and then they would ask me to stand up for ten minutes and study. That was a torture—just studying itself was a challenge, but to having to stand up was worse.

One way to miss these Studies sessions was to pretend to be sick and go to the hostel and sleep. But if the sickness was a bit more serious, then one would have to go to the sick room. Those who got headaches, coughs, or colds could stay in the hostel, while if you got fever, then you needed to go to the sick room.

I had used sickness as an excuse to skip Studies so frequently that most of the hostel masters and the sick room attendant knew my tricks. An older gentleman, coincidently called Sinniah, ran the sick room. We used to call him Dr. Kill. He was the real Dr. N. O. Know! It didn't matter what sickness you had; he would always prescribe vitamin C, maybe Disprin, and *kothamalli*, a local medicine. I had never seen him give out any other medicine, even if someone broke a leg.

I used to always go to him saying that I had fever and that I needed a pass to stay in the hostel. He got to know my plan and would send me back. I needed a new plan.

I went to him again.

"What is this time, *Thamby*? Fever?"

"No, Doctor, I think I got encyclopedia!"

"What?"

"Encyclopedia."

"Ummh…sounds like a serious issue. Let me check your pulse."

He did check my pulse while keeping his hand on my head. He told me to take two Disprins and to sleep for twelve hours.

That was my new plan—to use long English words to confuse him and get him to allow me to sleep in the hostel.

Another day, I went to him again. This time I wanted to try him out with something else. "Doctor, I think I need H_2O."

"What? How do you know that?"

"See these marks? They are because I need H_2O."

"You are so dark. I can't see any marks." He took my pulse again, gave me two Disprins, and told me to take a day off school and sleep.

We continued to go to church thrice a week, and I also converted these opportunities to catch up on my sleep. Every service had a sermon that we needed to listen to while seated. There was no one to test whether we listened to the sermon or not. That was one opportunity to fall asleep. There was another opportunity, as there was a long prayer after collections and before communion. We needed to kneel down and pray. I took advantage of that, too. Sometimes those in the choir who sat in front would notice those who were falling asleep. That didn't help my cause.

I was starting to have interest in girls, though there was no one in particular that I was keen on. My theory was to try to attract as many as possible, and someone would fall for me!

I now moved to Alison Hostel, which was closer to the toilets and to our bathing area. Our showers were made out of iron pipes, and most of them were rusty. You wouldn't shower standing close to these pipes. Every hosteller from the Memorial Block would pass Alison when they went to the showers and ended up having a chat with us through the windows.

Our week was always packed with activities. We had compulsory "resting time" during the weekends after lunch, and we had to be on our beds. We were allowed to read a book. I always started by reading a book and within minutes fell asleep. There were some who hardly slept and did all kinds of practical jokes. We would always target someone who was fast asleep and tie a rope to his leg, looping it through the leg of his bed, and finally tie the other end to his suitcase. The fun would begin when he woke up. He would definitely fall off the bed and pull his suitcase with him. It was a cruel joke, but we loved it.

I was now on to my O-level class. It was getting serious, as one had to pass the government exam at the end of the year to go to advanced levels. Success at A levels was essential, as that would then set us up for university.

I had set my goals. I planned to focus on four subjects for which I wanted to get credits. They were English, Christianity, physics, and pure mathematics. I could perhaps get a credit for applied mathematics and chemistry, but I knew that was tough. I was average in Tamil but should easily pass. Biology was a lost cause, and there was no way I could get even ten marks.

The worst-case scenario was four credits with three passes, and the best case was six credits and one pass. This would easily get me to A levels. The only thing on my mind was to get through. I knew that I could get through with the minimum. I studied the subjects I picked and went through past papers. I rarely listened to anything our teachers taught, as I was a daydreamer. I dreamt of a lot of things, including captaining the cricket team, going to the moon, bullfighting, and acting like MGR. I never could concentrate.

The pressure was building, and those who were not good enough tended to get up in the morning around five and study even before the rest of us woke up. Some would go for extra classes. I had none of that. I was not interested. I had a plan:

concentrate on four credits and three passes. It was that simple, and I stuck to it.

Mr. T. Sri Jeyakumar, our Alison Hostel master, was another handsome man. He was immaculately dressed. He wore different trousers from ours. His trousers were very tight and had pockets that were sewn horizontally rather than diagonally. I was determined to get some trousers made that way when I grew up.

Sir, like Mahendran master, was instrumental in our next drama. This time, we wrote a script called *Ottakapulagathar*. It was about a local Ayurvedic doctor. He was different from the other doctors and had no formal education in Western medicine. It was another hilarious performance.

Gopinath was the doctor, and I, his assistant. We put on one of the best dramas that I had ever witnessed. We had the audience laughing from the beginning to the end. Among the patients, we had a foreigner. It was, of course, Karthigesu, who was very fair but couldn't speak English well.

We won Best Drama and, to my total surprise, I won the Best Actor's Prize again. The judge commented that I had no stage fright. Really! He had no idea. I was so scared and worried before the drama began but started to feel at ease once we had the audience laughing. I had won the Best Actor's Prize two years in a row. It sealed me as an actor.

My nicknames were piling up: Visaran, Oothai, Alluppu, and Sorri. They were all related to my annoying jokes and painful comments.

Sir asked me to post a letter, and it was addressed to CGR: Ceylon Government Railways. He joined them soon after and left the college. We were all so fond of him. He was a very young guy, always laughing and joking with us. We had a very comfortable and close relationship with him. He could be very strict but was very humble and funny. We gave him a farewell party at the college tuck shop. That was a very sad day for us.

I was made captain of the hockey second team under Thevathasan master, and we had a very good season. We played seven matches and won six. I scored well and played as right in forward. One of my very good friends was the vice captain of the team. Once, we had a bad misunderstanding, and he refused to talk to me. I tried to speak to him, as I had been the one who annoyed and upset him. But he would not listen. He was the centre forward.

I decided to play a prank on him. I told the captain of Mahajana College that my vice captain was a bit mad and they should be very careful playing against him. I told him that my vice captain could go nuts and lash out at others, but he would never do that to anyone in his own team. He promptly told his coach, who then walked towards us. He spotted our coach and pulled him aside. "Sir, we can't be playing this match if you are going to let loose a mad boy. I can't risk my players."

"Oh, really? What are you talking about, Master?"

"I am told that your centre forward goes mad and starts attacking players."

"Who told you?"

I was praying that he would not mention my name, but he did. Thevathasan master walked towards me and shouted at me. He told me to apologize to the vice captain. I did, and we played the match.

I really enjoyed captaining the side, and we remained unbeaten. We didn't play all the matches against other schools but played some of the local clubs too. I had a wonderful team, and we really worked well together.

I used to go to the library every morning to read the newspapers. I had quietly developed an interest in football, and particularly Manchester United. I selected them as they had our college colours—red and black. All the newspapers would be placed on a stand at the back of the library. I would always start reading from the back page, which was the sports section. I followed club and school cricket and English football. The library was a very quiet place, and Miss Kararasingham, our librarian, kept it that way.

There was a light-blue magazine, *World Student News*, that had a lot of short articles about various subjects relating to students. I enjoyed them, as they were easy to read. I read about how friendships among students around the world were formed, and the magazine introduced the concept of pen pals. They interviewed students who discussed how they found pen pals. There was an interview with a Japanese guy, Akano Takita, and his Sri Lankan fiancée, Padma from Batticaloa.

I thought that this could be a good way of attracting a girl and then have the opportunity to marry her and move overseas. I sent my name to this magazine, and two months later, my name appeared. I had three letters.

The first one was from R. Ravi from Poona, India. He was similar age to me and was interested in cricket and movies. He and I corresponded for a few years, but it faded away.

The second one was from Albert J. Daufeldt from Iowa, United States. He was seventy-six years old and was involved in telecommunications. He and I corresponded a lot. He sent me caps, a shirt, and a rubber stamp with my name on it.

The last was from Mary Anne Cheung from Cebu, Philippines. She was three years older than me. We, too, wrote to each other a lot. She sent me a beautiful polo shirt and a tiepin engraved with my name.

I enjoyed the correspondence and waited for their letters to arrive. I learnt so much about their cultures and their interests and was always happy to receive photographs and the little gifts. I learnt a lot about their lives and surroundings.

I was now seriously eyeing a good-looking, quiet girl at church. She must have been two or three years younger than me. I did not know how to attract her or to approach her. My looks would not do. My studies would not do. My sporting abilities would not do. My best and perhaps only chance was to join the choir. The choir was already formed, and I knew she was on it. The only challenge was that I could not sing!

I went for the first choir practice. Mrs. Navaratnam brought some of the boys closer to the piano. "Please come one by one, as I need to decide."

Decide what? I thought. I was there to sing. *Do I need to do something else?*

Premkumar was first. "Ah, ah, ah…"

Mrs. Navaratnam asked him to repeat. He did that, and he was assigned to tenor. Ranjit and Ratnarajah were also assigned to tenor.

It was now my turn. "Ah, ah, ah…" Miss started.

"Oh, oh, oh…"

"No, I said, 'ah, ah, ah.'"

"Oooh, oooh, oooh…" I dragged it a bit to get that higher tone.

"Carefully repeat, Sinniah: ah, ah, ah."

My girl was seated in the front row and was looking down. She didn't even know I was singing. A blessing, I suppose.

"Eeeeeh, eeeeeeh…aaaah."

"Umm. Where shall we put you? Bass, I suppose."

"What is bass, Miss?"

"Another type of singing. You are a special case!"

Some people laughed, and I glanced at my girl in the front row. She was giggling with others. Perhaps she was happy that I joined, I encouraged myself.

Choir practices went on, and there were some songs I could sing well, but others were out of my range. The "Hallelujah" chorus was very difficult, nearing impossible.

Our carol service was one of the most exciting events. We practiced a lot. It made me avoid Studies, which suited me perfectly. This year's carol service was special. *She* was going to be there. I OCed Frank Samuel's St. Michael's shirt, and I had a pair of crimplin, blue trousers. There would always be a choir dinner after the carol service where all the choristers, boys and girls, met. At the dinner, we played some party games. I had to make the dinner so that I would get a chance to chat with that girl—my girl!

We all marched into the church in pairs. The girls went first, and then the boys followed, with the bass quartet at the end. It was actually a bass trio, as I hardly sang.

The carol service was going really well, and I was able to manage most of the songs. We all had to stand up after the blessings for the final song, the "Hallelujah" chorus.

One of the girls sang the first line beautifully, and then everyone in the choir joined in. There were a few lines that the bass got to do alone. The four of us sang, but I was not really singing. I just opened my mouth up and down without any noise for fear of spoiling the song. Miss, who was conducting, asked us to lift our voices. She kept on raising her hand, and I kept on raising my upper lip and then my mouth, and then did a full head up. There was nothing coming out of my mouth, and I didn't think she noticed.

After the carol service, we were all standing out and chatting, and I kept looking at my girl. Miss approached me. "Sinniah, how did that go?"

"Okay, Miss. I tried my best."

"But you didn't sing."

I knew I had been caught out. "I had a dry cough, and that didn't help."

"I think, let us be honest here. You are struggling to sing. Your brothers were great. I knew your mum could sing. Your Aunt Ranee is still a great singer. I thought you would be, too, but it doesn't seem to be. So, think of next year—you should focus on your studies rather than the choir."

It was a polite dismissal, but I was happy that I had made it this year. My main aim was to attend the dinner and speak to that girl.

Choir dinner was held at Williams Hall. Chairs were set up in a circle. The girls stood on one side, and the boys on the other. The girls came forward and put one of their shoes in the middle of this circle. They went back to their side, and the shoes were then mixed up.

The boys were now standing in a line, and when the priest gave us the go-ahead, we ran and picked a shoe. We walked around carrying the shoe until we found the girl it belonged to. The boy and girl would then be partners during the dinner. They could sit together for the whole evening.

What happened to me was another story.

My plan was to take that girl's shoe and sit next to her, but it was the same plan two other boys had. This competition I never knew of. Both my brothers had girlfriends, and I was convinced my time had come.

She had a pink-and-blue dress. She always dressed very simply and in pretty dresses. She was quiet and kept her eyes down. I felt she wanted me but was too shy to look at me. In Tamil, there was a saying that a girl always looked down when you stared at her but then looked up and smiled when you looked away.

I looked at her shoes. Her personality came through her shoes. She was wearing flat shoes in a light blue that matched her dress. I had a good look at her shoes. I wanted to make sure that I picked the right shoe.

I ran to get the light-blue shoe but, as always, was at the back of the rush. I didn't know, but some girls had already signalled to their boyfriends their shoe colour, make, and size. I never got that signal from my girl. By the time I got to the pile, the two boys were fighting over my girl's shoe, and one won the fight. He went straight to her and jubilantly declared, "I got it." She happily smiled and greeted him. I overheard her saying that she was very pleased. I knew that I had no chance and she was keen on someone else. I still had a shoe to match, though, and match I did!

My shoe matched a girl who was three years older than me. I went closer to her and showed her the shoe. "Oh, you. You got my shoe. This is my fate."

She was reasonably ugly, so I really didn't understand why she was not happy partnering me. "I will do my best."

"Did you put on any deodorant?"

"Yes, I put on some eau de cologne."

"God, it smells like Dettol."

She was livid. Her chance of finding a fine, young man was gone. A lot of girls walked past her and expressed their sympathy. "Oh, you got Oothai Sinniah. Ha, ha," and "Oh, you got Sorriyan. God will help you."

My dreams were crushed. The chance of me getting a girl in this environment was zero. I decided that I would make the best of the situation. This meant to act and behave like a fool. I did. There was a pass-the-parcel game, and when it came to me, I held it tight and wouldn't pass it on. We played musical chairs, and I pushed all, young and old, to get to the chair. And then, when the food was served, I ate like a pig and burped like one. I made sure my partner had a terrible night. I loved it. I had a good meal, messed up most of the games, and ensured she had a miserable time.

The ordinary-level exams were nearing. The official exams were held in December, and the results released in February. Our college had an exam called Withdrawals in November. If you passed Withdrawals, you went to A levels immediately in January and did not have to wait for the official results. However, if you failed Withdrawals, you had to stay back at Special Five (V).

The Withdrawals were a lot tougher than the official O levels, and no wonder I failed badly. My four-credits-and-three-passes strategy failed miserably, and I got only two credits and four passes. My parents were very angry and upset when they found out.

The O-level exams came. My strategy had not changed. I studied aiming for the same four credits and three passes and completely ignored biology.

The exams went according to plan, and biology was the last paper on the twenty-first. The paper was in the morning, and I was to leave for Dickoya on the night train. Whilst that was the exciting part, I knew I was in for a lambasting from my parents for failing the Withdrawals.

On the evening of the twentieth, everyone was studying hard for the biology exam, while I had no interest. I had a good shower and was sharing a joke with my hostel mates. Ganga, a friend of mine, told me that there was a new movie, *Mayangural Oru Madhu*, released for Christmas.

"Who is acting, *machchan*?"

"*Machchan*, Muthuraman, with a new actress."

"Really? Let us go."

"What about biology? You confident?"

"Oh, yeah, confident indeed."

"I have never met someone who is so confident that he doesn't want to study."

"Don't worry, *machchan*—everything will be all right."

We went together on his bicycle. We bought tickets for the gallery and some Bulto to eat.

The movie started in a girls' hostel. One of the girls was so innocent and sweet. She was shy and well behaved. She had beautiful, long hair. That was it. I fell in love with her and decided that I would go to Madras one day and marry her.

Sujatha!

This was supposedly her first movie. She was a stunning-looking girl. I decided I must see this movie again, perhaps the next day, before I went to Dickoya. This would cement her permanently in my mind. I went back to the hostel and went straight to bed.

"Get up! Get up! What are you mumbling?"

"Sujatha…Sujatha…Sujatha…"

"What? Who?"

"Oh God. Was I dreaming?"

I woke up, and there were only forty minutes to go before my biology paper. Everyone was ready, and most of them were praying really hard. I dressed up quickly and put a cross across my chest. I had planned to fail biology, but one never knows. They say God can do miracles.

The science subjects have all got two parts to the exams. The first part was a set of multiple-choice questions. Since I was the third child, I picked three as the answer for all the questions. That was done in two minutes instead of forty-five minutes.

The second part consisted of seven questions, and we needed to answer five. There was no reason to even read the question paper. The first question had a picture of a head with a brain whose parts were tagged A, B, C, D, E, and F. We had to name them. I drew the brain again on my answer sheet. I labelled them A, B, C, and D, and underneath that, I wrote:

$A = B = C = D$

I wrote that it was a beautiful brain and looked like a smart and intelligent one. I coloured part of the brain blue, as I was from Johnstone House. I also wrote that this could be a girl's brain because it was small.

I finished the paper in twenty minutes, and I put my hand up.

"What do you want?"

"I have finished answering."

"What?"

"I have finished the paper. Can I hand over my answer sheet and go?"

"No, you can't. You have to wait for at least thirty minutes. You can go after that."

Sir seemed annoyed. It was nine forty-five. The morning movie started at ten thirty in town. It would take me at least twenty minutes to go there by bus to see my darling Sujatha.

Exactly at the thirty minute cut-off, I handed over my answer sheet and went to the movie. I was late by ten minutes and missed the introduction where Sujatha was in the hostel, innocent and sweet. I was annoyed and grumbled a bit when someone next to me told me to be quiet.

I watched that movie again with one goal, and that was to get to India and marry her. I had won the Best Actor's Prize twice; it should be easy for me to get a role as a lead actor, act with her, and capture her heart. She was my dream girl now.

I got out of the cinema and bought a songbook that had her and Muthuraman on the cover. She was in a beautiful song in the movie. I kept singing all the way back to the hostel, "*Oru puram vedan, Maru puram nagam. Irrandukum naduave, azhagiya kalaiman, azhagiya kalaiman.*"

I was singing when someone knocked my head. I saw my friend Rajkumar. Achchi was laughing. "*Enna thamby, oru puram veddan, oh.*"

"This fellow is madly in love with Sujatha and watched one of her movies thirteen times. He even finished his O-level biology paper in twenty minutes to watch her first movie three years ago. Really a nutty Sujatha follower." Rajkumar was now talking to Achchi.

Why is he here? I wondered, as I wanted to continue to dream of Sujatha. All my secrets were now going to be revealed to Achchi. That's exactly what happened.

"What? He did O levels only three years ago? He said he is at the uni now."

"He is always joking. He just completed his A levels and is on his way back home. Chances of this fellow going to university is the same as me going to the moon."

"Oh, Kaduvale!" Achchi was calling God. "Why did he lie to me like this? I gave him food, barley, and some money, too. He is even using my pillow to sleep. Real *kallan*, *Thamby*." She was cursing me and called me a rogue.

"He is always joking. He is an innocent fellow." Rajkumar laughed and left. He had come to buy drinks at the train's buffet.

I felt so small and bad. The train stopped at Veyangoda, and it would be another hour before we reached Colombo. I gave the pillow back, and Achchi took it without saying a word.

It is true that I had watched the movie thirteen times in three months. I had Sujatha cemented firmly in my head and my heart, and everyone thought that I was so stupid to be in love with her.

I wanted to sleep again before we got to Colombo. I wanted to dream of Sujatha. I did fall asleep. I didn't dream of Sujatha.

THE ADVANCED LEVELS

MY PARENTS WERE SO ANGRY THAT I HAD FAILED THE WITHDRAWALS, BUT THEY WERE NOT AS HARSH AS I THOUGHT THEY WOULD BE. After the December holidays, I went to Special V, the repeat class. The results were due in six weeks, and I was completely bored being in that class.

I continued to dream of Sujatha. In our hostel, everyone had a picture of their religious beliefs on top of their beds. Some had Jesus, some had Murugan or Saraswathi, and some had other Hindu gods' statues or pictures. On top of my bed, I had Sujatha. I didn't worship her. I just adored her.

We were now in Crossette Hostel, the senior in the Memorial Block. Everyone was eagerly awaiting the O-level results. It was a tough six-week period. Almost all who were in the Special V class were expected to fail and to repeat O levels.

The day of the results came. Sriharan master asked me if I could do him a favour. I was waiting for the results, but he reminded me that they would be released only after eight. He was getting married and needed someone to help carry his *thallapa*, the headgear worn at Hindu weddings, to his home. I was fine by this and sat behind him in his scooter.

We turned into his lane, with me holding on to this precious parcel at the back, when a dog started barking. I like dogs and started smiling at it when it licked me. Then it started to bark and tried to bite me. I had to raise both my legs, and Sriharan master lost control of his scooter. We swayed from left to right and right to left and finally came to a stop at his gate. He was a bit annoyed but saw the funny side of it. We went back to college just before eight.

The results normally came by the mail train. The principal and the vice principal would have a quick look at them and then release them to the students. The train was very late, and there was no sign of the results. Around eight thirty, I saw Amarasingham master walking out of the office, and I knew the results would be out soon. I was very nervous and shaking inside. The good students were all very relaxed and chatting. I didn't joke that day. All I wanted was to get to A levels.

I went past Mr. Nadarajah's desk—he was our welfare office clerk—and looked up at the list of names. The results were pasted on the wall:

B. S. Sinniah S C C F S C C S

"Oh, yeah. Oh, yeah." I didn't shout out loud but mumbled softly to myself. I went out of the office and then back again. I checked my name once more.

B. S. Sinniah…

I paused, took a foot ruler, and lined up my name against the results:

B. S. Sinniah S C C F S C C S

I was thrilled. I threw the ruler on the floor and walked confidently to my classmates. They looked surprised. Ganga came, wanting to know my results, and I told him proudly, "Four credits and three passes."

"Let me guess—you failed biology, right?"

"Yeah, I must have missed that by one mark."

"What? You left the hall in thirty minutes, and you expected to pass?"

"Never mind, *machchan*. I passed, and on to A levels, man."

I was so happy. All those boarders who got their results were allowed to go out of college and do whatever they wanted. Karthigesu and I went to the post office and sent telegrams to our parents.

Passed O levels. Four credits and three passes.

Chooty

We both decided that we should go and see a movie. I suggested a movie that Sujatha starred in—*Aval Oru Thodar Kathai*. Karthigesu rejected it. He wanted to see an English movie. There were a lot of posters next to Kachcheri Bus Stand. We found that *The Arena* was being screened at Rio. This show was of particular interest because it was classified as adults only.

"*Machchan*, let us go and see this."

"Why?" I asked.

"Adults only, *machchan*. Never seen one before." Karthigesu was pleading. I got convinced.

We went to Rio. We bought second-class seats. The movie was very boring. It may have been classified as adults only, but nothing got us excited. We were so angry. We started talking to each other about it, and in fact, most of the people there were doing the same. They were all annoyed. We came to the last scene, and I told Karthigesu that we should leave. As we were leaving, they showed a girl slowly taking her top off, and then the movie ended. We should have been very happy because of our test results, but we were very angry because of this stupid movie.

The results were exactly as I had planned, and I decided that I must construct another plan for advanced levels. I knew I was poor at biology. I knew I did badly at biology. I knew I hated biology. Even after all that, I decided I should become a doctor. Why not? One could always improve. I now wanted to become a doctor!

I went on to A-level classes. Everyone in my class, including the teachers, was shocked that I joined the Bio stream. "Are you sure?" "You thought about this?" "You up for it?" "You are mad!" "You are stupid!" "You were crap at biology." These were the comments I heard from all. I was determined.

The first few classes went well, and we went to the Zoology Laboratory. Miss Rajasingham walked in. She was very attractive and had long hair, but my heart was already lost to Sujatha, and I never stopped thinking of her.

Miss gave us a frog. It was already dissected. "Students, look at this frog. It has been dissected. Let me see you draw this on your note pads. Let me take it from there. I will give you fifteen minutes to do it."

I didn't know where to start. *Do I start drawing from the head or from the legs? Should I draw the dissected body first?* I drew it. It took about ten minutes. I admired my piece of art.

Miss went around, giving comments and patting some on the shoulders. She came to my table. She looked at my drawing. She turned the book upside down and stared hard. She looked at it from all angles. "Really? Sinniah, this is a masterpiece. I have never seen anyone draw a small frog that turned out like a goat! You need to draw this again. You are going to be severely tested. You need to get this right."

It was there and then I decided that Bio stream was not for me. I had to get out of any bio subjects like zoology and botany. I walked straight from the class to the principal's office. As he was busy, I spoke to Mr. Amarasingham. He asked me about my first day. I told him of my decision. He couldn't believe that I even contemplated doing zoology. He was my biology teacher and knew that I was a disaster.

I spoke to the principal, who completely supported my decision, and I moved to the Mathematics stream immediately. I would study four subjects for my A levels—pure mathematics, applied mathematics, physics, and chemistry. I quickly settled down in the class and did reasonably well.

I continued to think of Sujatha. My friends advised that it would be very difficult for me to find an acting role in Madras and to focus on a local girl.

Lower VI was very good fun. The Mathematics stream had only about twenty-four students. During the year, some of them left for England to do a Higher National Diploma (HND), while some went to Colombo. Aso left us and went to India. He was a very bright student, and I had grown up with him from fourth grade. We were left with sixteen students, and all of them were bright except two, and I was one of those.

Our timetable for Lower VI had a lot of free study periods that were supposed to be used for revision. We used that time to sing old Tamil songs and used the tables as drums. In one of our weekly literary meetings, we had a small drama. I was not involved, but I was determined to disturb it. That was my style.

The drama started, and within the first two minutes, I stood up and told them to stop. Our patron, Mr. Ganeshalingham, asked me why I was doing that. "Sir, in a meeting, the two most important people are the president and the secretary—both of them are blocked by these actors. I can't see them."

"Why is it important?"

"Sir, come on, Sir. Very important."

"Okay, this is stupid, but anyway, the president and the secretary can come here and sit next to me." He invited them closer to him.

The drama continued and went on for another three minutes before I stood up again.

"Now what, Sinniah?"

"Sir, now I can't figure out who the patron is."

"What, come again?"

"Now I cannot figure out who the patron is, Sir."

"Really? You do not know who I am because they are sitting next to me? Okay, let me show you who I am. I will make sure you know who I am. The actors, please go back to your seats. President and secretary, please go to the front. I will show him who I am." He turned towards me. "You, Sinniah, come here. I, K. Ganeshalingham, am the patron!" He was shouting, "Do you really want to know me? Do you really want to know me?" He took his ring off his finger and started slapping me on both cheeks. He really hammered me. "Now, do you know me?" He slapped me again. "Do you know me? Tell me, yes or no?"

After a few minutes, he asked me to get back to my seat. He was still shaking. I had really upset him, otherwise a very quiet and calm man, and made him lose his temper.

Boarding life continued to be great. The school arranged films to be played in our college hall. We would watch a documentary, a sporting event, and then a movie. We watched the tied test between Australia and West Indies in 1960, over and over again. We watched numerous Charlie Chaplin movies.

The boarders were notorious for jumping over the college wall and stealing bananas, coconuts, and other foods from the neighbours' gardens. We always planned the attack after everyone had gone to sleep. We did this for a few months, until one day, a dog started to bark.

The three of us who were in the garden had started to climb the wall back to school when the dog got hold of Ravi's legs. It bit him, and he was bleeding profusely. We had no choice but to take Ravi to the sick room. We saw a few hostel masters seated in front of Fleming Hostel, having a chat.

"What are you all doing?" asked N. R. Arumainayagam master.

"Sir, taking Ravi to the sick room."

"Why?"

"Dog bit him, sir."

"Dogs? There are no dogs here. What are you all talking about?"

The other masters joined him, and they walked towards us. In the rush, we had forgotten to leave the three coconuts and bananas back in the hostel, and they saw that Karthigesu was still carrying them. "Where did you get this stuff?" Manikavasagar master chipped in.

"Sir…Sir…"

"Leave it here." He took the stuff and asked us to get Ravi to the sick room. Karthigesu and I were holding him, and he was in serious pain. The masters didn't say anything, but they took the coconuts and the bananas.

We always hosted the Jaffna Talent Contest, a musical competition organized by the YMCA. It was always held on a Saturday. I was not a musical person, and I knew very few English songs. I knew only one song by heart from a movie Sujatha starred in.

Whenever the talent contest was held, all the young girls from various schools came over. That was the only reason I went for these programmes. I continued dreaming of Sujatha, but that other girl I liked continued to come to church and continued to look pretty. I looked at her all the time, but I got no signals from her. I mentioned her to a lot of people, but no one thought I had any chance.

Our principal retired, and Mr. Anandarajan replaced him. We held a lot of events to celebrate the retirement and to welcome the new principal. The boarders had a function, and I was selected to give a speech. I OCed Thayalan's white shirt and Ravi's trousers. I had a pair of socks that was washed and clean. Binco, a new type of shoe, was becoming very popular. It was made of plastic and had small holes underneath. My shoes were dark blue.

I walked from Crossette to the dining room for the function. My Bincos kept collecting stones. By the time I got to the dining room, there were about six small stones stuck under my shoes.

The senior boarding master called my name. I walked from the back of the dining room to the front. The stones stuck underneath my shoes made a lot of noise. I was in serious pain and hated those Bincos.

I gave a decent speech and made about three jokes about the former and current principals. That was my first public speech ever, and I felt very satisfied with myself. I walked back in serious agony. It was very sad to see the principal retire.

Lower VI had their own college social. Ramanan, Shanthi, Mahendran, and I were put in charge of the lighting, and we named ourselves the "Lighting Committee." We hardly did anything but used the time to chat and went to Subhas Café to have Chinese rolls and ice cream. On the day of the social, however, we did deliver the right lighting.

Mr. S. S. Manuelpillai, our patron, asked me to be the master of ceremonies. The social was well attended by students' representatives from other schools in Jaffna. I made a lot of mistakes, even though I had written down everything. After the social, Sir congratulated me on a job well done and asked me how I felt. I said I felt nervous and that I missed a lot of things that I had wanted to say.

"See, Sinniah, this you must learn. Never worry if you miss something. There is only one person who would know that, and that is you. No one knew what you were supposed to say. Therefore, if you miss something, don't worry. The main thing is to prepare and practice your speech and make sure you remember the key points."

It was a great lesson.

"By the way if you are keen, you can join my evening Spoken English classes. Let me know."

I did join his class. The first day was comical. He wanted us to get our pronunciation right.

"Okay, repeat after me. All of you…say, 'Come again…come again.'"

We repeated. He was not happy. We said it over one hundred times. He was getting irritated. He started clapping: "When I clap, say, 'C-A.' Next clap, I want to hear 'U-M.' Next clap, 'A,' and then 'gain.' This is very simple, but we can't move on from here unless you get it right."

We did this for the next forty minutes. He kept clapping, and we kept saying, "Come again." He was exhausted, and we were too. I couldn't figure out the issue, but he was not satisfied. He said that we should have a break and start again next week. I never went to that class again.

I got my dad to pay for some extra mathematics tuition from Easan master. The first few classes were great. They were held next to Lido Cinema, and it always screened the latest Tamil movies. I was tempted to go there, but I resisted it.

I did well until I passed by Sridhar Theatre one day. What I saw there put an end to my tuitions. There was a huge cardboard cutout of Sujatha, my sweetheart. She was in a new movie called *Annakilli*. She was acting alongside Sivakumar, the hero of the snake movie. I let the bicycle turn into Sridhar. I sat nicely in the gallery. There weren't many people, and that was odd, as it was a new movie.

The movie started. It wasn't my Sujatha. It wasn't *Annakilli*. It was *Neerkumili*. It was an old movie, and I had seen it before. I was furious, but the doors were closed, and one had to walk right back to access the main door. I sat and watched until halftime. I asked the man at the ticket counter, "What, no *Annakilli*? No Sujatha?" He looked at me in total disbelief and asked me whether I had read the poster. He didn't say much.

I went out and read the poster. *Annakilli* was going to be released in two weeks' time. I left the cinema and went straight to Mokkan Kadai and had a *koththu roti*.

Two weeks later, I skipped tuition and went straight to Sridhar, confirmed that *Annakilli* was screening, and watched it alone. She was mine, and I wanted to be alone with her. It was a brilliant movie, and Sujatha was again so innocent and nice. She had long hair, sang songs while running around trees, and fell in love with Sivakumar. I got so excited whenever she appeared on screen. I watched that movie seventeen times in the next three months. I did that during my tuition classes. I watched the first few times properly. Later on, I would fall asleep until she appeared in that beautiful song—"Annakilli Unnai Theduthey." After that, I would dream of her singing to me and begging me to marry her.

Premkumar's uncle was at the Tamil section of the Sri Lanka Broadcasting Corporation. There was a programme called *Indreya Neyar* where a chosen listener requested three songs. It was our national broadcaster, and it was difficult to get onto these programmes. Premkumar's influence got me in. I requested three songs, and all were from the movies that Sujatha acted in. The programme was broadcasted on a Wednesday at five fifteen in the evening.

We were all glued to the radio when Sylvester M. Balasubramaniam announced that the chosen fan was going to be B. S. Sinniah. I was so thrilled to hear my name. He pointed out that all three songs were from movies that Sujatha had acted in and that B. S. Sinniah must be a hard-core Sujatha fan. I was now doubly thrilled. I knew that SLBC Tamil Service was being broadcast to South India.

"*Machchan*, Premkumar. Will Sujatha be listening to this?"

"Yes, man. The famous Sujatha is going to sit next to the radio and will be waiting to hear this. Just stop this nonsense and study hard." Premkumar was a brilliant student, especially in mathematics.

At the school holidays, we did not go to Dickoya, as Mummy had an operation in Colombo. We all went and stayed with my aunt, Baby Marmie, in Mutuwal. I went to see Mummy at the hospital and felt sad, as she was in pain. I did visit her a few times, but my eyes were on a new movie—*Apoorva Ragangal.*

Loga Acca had some good friends called the Rajasinghams. They had a few children, but I was close to Rajboy, their son. Sutha Acca and Thanga, his sisters, would join us to watch the latest Tamil movies. We did watch *Apoorva Ragangal*, but to my disappointment, it was not a Sujatha movie. Still, we had so much fun going in the bus from Mutuwal and watching movies at so many different local cinemas. I was crazy for movies.

One day when I went to see Mummy at the hospital, she complained, "Where have you been? Everyone else has been coming to see me in the mornings and evenings, but you are not to be seen. You don't visit me enough."

I felt really down. I was sad that I did this to Mummy, but movies seemed to be more important in my life. "You know, Mummy, I am now in A levels, and studies are becoming difficult. I am studying, and that is why I have been unable to come here to see you."

"Really? Do you think I am that stupid? Loga tells me you have been going for a lot of movies. Why do you need to lie?"

Fortunately for me, some more people came to see her just then. I bent and kissed her on her cheeks and went for another movie. After the holidays, Mummy went back to Dickoya, and we went back to college.

The Boarders' Day was on, but we failed to produce a good drama. We left it too late to prepare. I participated in the fast eaters' competition. While everyone was eating fast to win the competition, I took my own time and had a good meal. Ponniah master was so upset and called me a "dog in a manger." He scolded me for depriving another boy of a chance to compete and win. "Whatever. I had a great meal. Half a pound of bread with beef! I never had it before," I mumbled, and walked away satisfied.

Boarding food was never the best. We were always left hungry and took to the tuck shop to have something extra. The budget was very limited. We were not allowed to keep cash in the hostel and only had coupons. The schoolmasters had accounts at the tuck shop, and so did some of the senior boys. I was not that senior yet, and my coupons were running out fast. I was desperate for extra food, and by midweek, I would have no coupons left.

I approached the manager. He was a very holy man, with a lot of holy ash on his forehead. He had joined only about a few weeks ago and was struggling to differentiate the students and masters. I started singing a few songs and gave him the impression that I had joined the school recently as a music teacher. I told him that I was twenty and had graduated from Annamalai in India. He was very impressed. "What is your name, Sir?"

"Arumanayagam," I replied.

"Ah, I see you have an account, and it seems you very rarely use it."

"Yeah, but now I am going to use it regularly," I said to him confidently.

"What do you want, Sir?" He was so polite.

"One Chinese roll and a cake, please."

"Tea or coffee?"

"No, I drink only water. It helps with my singing," I lied confidently and out of hunger.

I used this account very frequently, including to buy food for my friends. The manager reminded me that I owed the tuck shop ten rupees. I kept going and was reminded that I had crossed thirty rupees. I was worried, but I kept going.

I didn't realize that the accounts were passed over to the individuals to settle at every month's end. The details went to Arumanayagam master, and he protested to the manager. I was found out, but fortunately, he didn't report me to the principal. He asked me to settle the account within a month. I paused my chemistry tuitions by VTK for a few months and settled it.

I was now in Upper VI. A levels would be in twelve months' time. Time flew by us, and it was getting stressful. It didn't stop us from having fun. Life was great. Studies were smooth, as I made no effort.

M. S. Chinniah and I were very close friends. He was very dark and was aptly nicknamed Karri, and I continued to be called Sorri. We were always joking around and annoying people. Some found it very irritating, but that never stopped us.

We were chatting after breakfast on a Saturday when we saw a tall white man talking to our gatekeeper, Benedict, and then walk towards Williams Hall. We were getting ready to go for the second Studies. I asked M. S. whether he knew the white man. He had no idea, but we both agreed that we must chat with him. That was our style. We poked our noses into everything that was happening.

We approached him. The white man was wearing a long shirt, not tucked inside his trousers, with a brown hat and a long beard. We introduced ourselves.

"I have come to visit this prestigious school. I am an American, and here is my card." We looked at it. He was a professor of some university, and underneath his name, he had the words "Fulbright Professor." He kept looking at the college bell that was hanging next to the office. He was taking some photographs.

"*Machchan*, Karri. What is 'Fulbright Professor'?"

"Sorri, I think 'Fulbright' means he is fully bright—a really bright chap."

We both decided that we could never be Fulbright. M. S. and I spoke to each other in Tamil.

"What do you want to see here, Professor?" I asked him.

"We can show you around, Sir," M. S. joined.

I knew M. S. was not keen on Studies; neither was I. We were thrilled when the professor accepted our offer. We ran to Gnanam Anna, who was in charge of Second Studies, and told him that we needed to take this white man around. We took him around the college and showed him various buildings and introduced him to a few people: "He is a bright boy and is studying to become a doctor. His name is Suthendran." That was a lie. The guy had no chance of even passing his O levels.

We introduced another guy: Thambirajah. "This boy is Sri Lanka's number one in weight lifting." That was another lie. He was just very fat. We lied about everything and enjoyed it.

The professor took about two hours to tour the school, taking a lot of notes. Three weeks later, at the college assembly, the principal announced that he had received several books from a professor who had come to visit us. "The professor was very grateful to two students—M. S. Chinniah and B. S. Sinniah. These books will be kept in the library. Thank you to both these students. He also sent a special book on medicine and another on weightlifting to two specific students. I will confirm these names with the professor and announce them next week."

After the assembly, the principal called M. S. and me into his office. He said we did a great job and that the professor was very grateful. "Well done. But I am bit confused with these two other books. What is this about? He says to give this medicine book to Suthendran so that he will succeed in medicine. He still hasn't got through his second attempt at O levels. We don't even have weightlifting at college, but Thambirajah has got a book on that. Explain to me so that I can write back."

M. S. looked at me, and I looked at him. We just stared at the principal.

"You think I don't know or can't work it out? You have both lied about these guys, right? You need to be more responsible. Anyway, it was a funny joke, but don't get too carried away." We were both relieved, as we thought he would punish us.

We continued to have so much fun at boarding, though we gave up climbing over the wall and going into our neighbours' houses to steal coconuts and bananas after the dog episode.

Tharmu came out with a new plan. He told us that he saw a beautiful bunch of bananas inside the college. Surrounding the science lab, there was a small park. The electrician, Selvaratnam, was living there and was responsible for the security. Inside this park, there were rare plants that were used for the botany lab. There was a small fish pond and a banana tree. None of us dared to go near this tree, as Selvaratnam would report us to the principal.

"No, *machchan*. It is easy," Tharmu assured us.

"We would be kicked out of the school if we get caught." Sivasothy was reluctant.

"Where can we hide this big bunch of bananas? It will take about two weeks to eat them all." I was nervous. There was no way we could hide them inside our hostels.

"Okay, I got a plan. The Handy Hostel master's room is not occupied. Let us hide them there. No one would check that room. We can leave them there." Tharmu was keen.

"And then what? How you plan to eat them?" Sothy was scared.

K. K. joined us now. "Let us do it." He was also keen.

"Stupid fellow. Just wait. We will all be sent out of school." Sothy was adamant that we should not do it.

"What I will do is go to the room every day, take a few bananas out, put them in my cloth bag, and take it home. In the nights, I will bring it back to the dining room, and we can eat them." Joshua, my cousin who was the senior prefect, came out with this master plan. As the senior prefect, he could go out of college anytime. Therefore, this arrangement suited him. "Let us do it. Sothy, just relax and let us make this happen. A good challenge, and this Selvaratnam needs to be stirred up, as he never allows us to get into his park."

I was encouraging. K. K. and Tharmu were fine too, and Sothy now joined in.

We were all college prefects and were supposed to be responsible. Tharmu was the prefect at Handy, and it was convenient to hide these bananas in that room. We did take the bananas from the park. We took them to Handy Hostel's master's room. Joshua did his daily visits to Handy, and Tharmu kept giving him small bunches of bananas. Joshua took the bag home and brought it back. The operation was going smoothly, but there were a lot of bananas to eat.

Selvaratnam did not realize that this all happened until the third day. He ran to the principal and complained to him. The principal marched towards the dining room. He approached me. I was nervous. "Sinniah, some fools have stolen those bananas. They shouldn't do that. We are experimenting something with those bananas, and they don't know the value of it. It has to be these senior fellows. Useless fellows."

"Yes, Sir. Very bad people." I marched behind him.

The principal trusted the prefects and would never suspect us. "Someone has taken the bananas," he said. "We need to know who did it. Otherwise, we will do a hostel-by-hostel search. I will suspend you unless you admit it now!" Principal was angry and was screaming in the dining room. Everyone was quiet, and I was standing behind him. "Right, Sinniah, bring some prefects, and we will go and search. You pick three or four."

"Sure, Sir. K. K., Sothy, and Tharmu, can you join me?"

Joshua had just arrived from home and joined us too. We searched every hostel and every room, including where the cooks slept. The cooks were so upset. Chelliah, our head cook, complained that it was terrible to suspect them.

"No chance; everyone will be searched." K. K. was talking boldly.

None of the boarding masters' rooms were checked. The principal gave up. "Thank you. I am sorry for taking you all out of your study time. I really appreciate it. Let it go."

We were so happy but felt very bad that he suspected everyone else but us. I felt particularly down when he checked the cooks' quarters.

Some of us became very good and close friends. Frequently, some of them would get food parcels from their relatives, and they would always share and eat. We all shared everything unconditionally.

Manikavasagar master and Karunanayagam master took a few of us to Karainagar on a Saturday. We had a good sea bath at Casurina Beach and went to Selvarajah's house for lunch.

The two masters, in the meantime, went out to a toddy tavern. Selvarajah took the chance to let us taste Karainagar toddy. We got very drunk but managed to keep a straight face, though two of the boys started vomiting when the two masters came in. They were angry with us but were themselves a bit tipsy. They helped us to clean the two boys, and we went back to the hostel. The two were sick for a week.

OC was still rampant, and almost everyone did it. One day, I borrowed Nirmalanda's nice, pink shirt and wore it to church. I was very pleased, as it was a brand-new one. I folded the shirt nicely after church and put it back in his cupboard. I didn't want him to know that I had worn it. "*Madayan*, why did you take my shirt?" Nirmalanda was so angry that Kethees had to hold him down. "My father gave me that shirt for my birthday next week. You ruined it, you fool!"

He was calling me all sorts of names. I apologized and walked away. Once something was worn, others could wear it, as well. Joshua, my cousin, didn't know that I had already worn this shirt to church. He wore the same pink shirt to church the following Sunday.

Shalini was with us at Youth Fellowship. She noticed it. "Interesting. Last week, Chooty wore it, and now you. Whose shirt is it?"

Before I could jump in and say something, Joshua quickly responded. "Ah, Chooty, *aiyoo*. He wears all my clothes. Do you like the shirt?"

I didn't want to let Joshua down but I heard Shalini saying, "How can anyone wear that shirt after Chooty wore it? Oothai Sinniah…ha, ha, ha, ha, ha!" Joshua never wore that shirt again.

The Interact Club was very active, and I was their treasurer. We organized a lot of events and were put in charge of the car park at the Saint Patrick's carnival. The movie *The Party*, with Peter Sellers, was organized by us and a brilliant success.

I still had no girlfriend and had given up on that girl in the choir. While I never knew whether she liked me or not, I knew the family would never allow her to even think of me.

The church organized their annual sale during the third term. The SCM camps in Casurina Beach, in Kayts, and in Navajeevanam presented us with more opportunities to meet and interact with girls. I went for all of these camps and OCed my friends' decent clothes and tried to always look good. But nicknames like Oothai Sinniah, Sorri Sinniah, and Visaran Sinniah didn't help. None of the girls wanted to be associated with a boy with all these nicknames. As my inferiority complex kicked in, I had now all but given up on any girl within the Chundikuli community.

It was now that I was presented with an amazing opportunity. Every school had a college dinner. To these dinners, two representatives from each school in Jaffna were invited. Everyone wanted to go to our sister school's dinner. Two best students were normally chosen, and I had zero chance of being nominated. Uthaya, who was the president of the A-level union, suggested that I go for the Holy Family Convent dinner. Convent is a Catholic girls' school. I knew the girls would be very conservative and that none of the boys would be allowed to sit next to the girls. I was sure that the nuns would be on full alert. But it was worth a try!

I did OC and wore a pair of lovely blue trousers paired with a clean, white shirt and a red-and-black tie. I went with another Johnian called Shan. The president of their A-level union warmly welcomed us. She introduced me to the committee and told us to just mingle and feel at home, as official proceedings would start later. I was talking to some of the girls, and I knew none of them.

I saw the back of a girl with beautiful, long hair. Her figure reminded me of Sujatha. I didn't listen to what was being said to me. I was focused on her. She did not turn and wasn't looking in my direction. She was wearing something very blue. I was convinced she was for me. I loved blue, and it was my Johnstone House colour. *Make or break. I have got nothing to lose.*

I excused myself when I saw Ramani. I knew Ramani from Easan master's tuition. She approached the blue girl and was talking to her when I interrupted them. It was "Sujatha." That beautiful, innocent smile. She had a pointed, pretty nose and a small nose stud. "Hi, Ramani. How are you? Still going to Easan master?"

"Hi, Sinniah. How are you? Yes, but looks like you have given up your studies." That was the last thing I wanted to hear in front of the blue girl.

"No, and I don't want to sound arrogant, but my teacher told me that I am doing very well and that I don't need to go for tuitions. Whether I get ninety or ninety-five, doesn't really make a difference, eh?" Blue girl turned and smiled.

Should I introduce myself or not? I wondered. "Hi. From St. John's."

"Yes, I know. I think I am sitting next to you."

I couldn't believe my luck, and I couldn't talk. "I…I…I…I hope so. You seem to be a happy person."

"Ha, ha…what are you studying?"

Ramani left us and went off. Blue girl and I were now alone. I could smell the flowers on her hair. Sujatha was definitely in front of me. I always liked simple faces with simple, pleasant looks. Some people thought I liked *pavam* (sad) faces, but I only liked Sujatha faces.

I was struggling to talk, but she spoke a lot. She seemed to be doing well at school, and I, of course, told her the truth. I didn't want to lie to Sujatha. I told her that I was struggling except for applied mathematics. She was such a nice girl; she didn't harp on my studies.

A nun came out and told us that the official event was starting, and we all went in. This was my day, and I sat next to Sujatha. She was very talkative but a bit shy. I was normally an extravert, but that night, I just sat there and listened to her. I didn't talk to any of the girls that were seated around me. Who would forgo a chance to talk to Sujatha? I asked her if she had seen *Annakilli*. She was not interested in movies. I bluntly told her that she looked like Sujatha and that I was in serious love with Sujatha. I was hoping that she would pick up my hint, but I was not sure.

She and I had dinner, and our plates were taken off. She was very religious and went to Saint Anthony's Church every Tuesday. That was so convenient, as Tuesdays were my tuition day for physics at Gnanam master's. I wished her well and told her I hoped to see her soon. She wished me well, too. There was no shaking hands, but I waited until she turned and walked. Sujatha's hair, Sujatha's figure, Sujatha's walk, and it was Sujatha. She was for me.

I went to Saint Anthony's every Tuesday for two months, but I never, ever saw her. I never even asked her name. I gave up and went back to dreaming of Sujatha. A new movie of Sujatha, *Andaman Kathalli*, had just been released. I watched it nine times.

Uthaya asked me to go for the Mahajana dinner with Jeyakumar. We took a bus from Kachcheri to Jaffna. When we got down from the bus, Jeyakumar politely reminded me, "*Machchan*, you know this is a vegetarian dinner."

"What—don't be stupid. A vegetarian dinner?"

"Yes, *machchan*. Don't you have brains? It is a strong Hindu school. That is their tradition."

"*Machchan*, I am out. Let us eat *koththu roti* here and go back to the hostel." I had made my decision.

"Sure—I agree," said Jeyakumar.

We were walking towards Mokkan Kadai when we saw a poster.

HARAN THEATRE
Screening Sivaji in a Bhimsingh movie
PANTHA PASAM

We decided to go there immediately. It was a very old but legendary film. It was being shown after fifteen years. We watched the movie, had our *koththu roti*, and went back to college. No one ever knew what really happened and that we didn't attend Mahajana's dinner.

Johnstone continued to perform well but never achieved top two. We would always finish third. My very good friend Shanthy became our house captain. He called for a strategy meeting at the tuck shop. There were five of us: Shanthy, Uthaya, Anpalagan, Kethees, and myself. He wanted us to help him win this year. We all agreed.

He made me the treasurer. We collected two rupees from each Johnstone houseboy, and the masters gave us ten rupees each. We had a decent amount of money to spend. Every athlete was fed glucose before he took part in an event and then again after the event. I had to buy many boxes of glucose.

Our strategy to get Johnstone from third to first was abandoned halfway. It never worked. We ended up using the money at Cheryl's Café opposite the school to eat *koththu roti* and *adai* with plain tea. When Shanthy became suspicious about my glucose distribution, I had to tell him the truth that we had spent it all at Cheryl's and didn't have any funds to buy glucose.

I participated in three-thousand- and five-thousand-metre track events and got second place in both, behind Mayooran. I was pleased, as I got into the college athletic team.

Anpalagan was a great athlete, and his strengths were in the field events. He was our only hope at winning discus and javelin. Every house had to field two athletes in every event, and both had to qualify to generate points. We found someone to partner Anpalagan in discus, but we couldn't find one for javelin.

"Sinniah, can you throw?" Shanthy asked me.

"Throw what?"

"Javelin."

"No, I can't."

"Hey, just throw it and make sure that the tip of the javelin lands first. There is no qualifying distance, and all you have to do is just get it right. Anpalagan will do the rest and win the event.

We will get his points." I knew that they were not banking on my points but only wanted me to throw properly so that we got his points.

The event started, and it was my turn to throw. I ran hard, crossed the line, and forgot to release the javelin. For the second try, Shanthy gave me a lot of glucose. He gave a kick on my backside and told me to concentrate. I ran fast, completely stopped at the line, and dropped the javelin slowly. I made sure the tip of the javelin touched the ground first. I did qualify, and the distance was an impressive two yards.

Ponniah master was angry and shouted at me, "You are a fool and are depriving others from participating. Yes, you qualify, but even a two-year-old can throw that far. That is not the spirit."

"But, Sir, aren't they the rules?"

"You are a lost cause—go away."

We got the points of Anpalagan but still came fourth overall.

During the December holidays, I decided to stay in Chundikuli and study for my A levels, which was three months away. I rented a room down Somasundaram Avenue together with Gopinath. We had to give one rupee per day to Mrs. Aiyathurai, who was the owner of the house. She had a helper called Appah, and he gave us coffee and tea for that one rupee. We would walk along the railway line and go to YMCA to eat. She didn't provide us with meals. Mrs. Aiyathurai had a piano, and a few girls would go there to practice.

Gopinath and I normally ate our dinner early, around seven, and then walk back to our place. Along the way, we would think of going for a movie. We rarely watched any movies in the first week and really concentrated on our studies. By the second week, we were bored with our studies and tuitions. We were now dying to go for movies.

We would toss a coin: heads, we would go for movies, and tails, we would study. We would keep tossing until we got heads. In the thirty-three days at Mrs. Aiyathurai's house, we watched twenty-one movies. At times, we watched two movies a day. I rarely went for tuitions either, and I was seriously behind in my study plan.

The A-level exam was nearing, and my best possible results would be four passes. The grading for A levels was different from that of O levels; A was a Distinction, B was a Very Good Credit, C was for Credit, and S was a Pass, while F was a Fail.

My aim was to get four Ss, although three Ss would get you through A levels. This was my first attempt, and that was what I aimed for. I completely concentrated on practicing past A-level papers and would do them repeatedly.

Panckyachelvan was one of the best students at the hostel, and he entered the medical faculty. They said that he could study really well because he shook his legs a lot while he studied. Sothy told me that I should try, as it seemed to have worked for him. I did try but fell asleep within minutes. I tried every possible tactic to concentrate on my studies but failed miserably.

I got three passes. I failed in chemistry. I decided to do A levels again, which was going to be held in six months. I made a decision that I would study hard. I had made these resolutions before but never held on to any.

The Jaffna schools sports meet took place at Central College grounds. I took part in the three- and five-thousand-metre races. I came in third in the three thousand and was quite excited to participate in these long-distance events.

The announcement was made that the five thousand would start in two minutes. I walked with Mayooran to the starting line, and to my amazement, there were only two participants. We were both from St. John's. Mayooran took off, and I decided to just relax and take my time. I was guaranteed a second place. I did get the second prize, but only after Mayooran had a three-lap lead over me.

Ponniah master was there again. Furious! Blasted at me once more. "You are a disgrace to the college. You did it with javelin, and now here, in front of all schools. I am glad you are leaving the school soon."

I stayed back from going to Dickoya for Xmas. I signed up for tuitions for all four subjects but in truth hardly went.

Sujatha's new movie, *Uyanthavargal*, was released at Sridhar Cinema, and I watched it eleven times. There was another great movie, *Moondru Mudichchu*, that was being screened at Windsor, and I watched it nine times. My studies just suffered.

My good friend Mohan moved from Chava to Chundikuli. I was very friendly with him and got closer to his family. His sister needed some help with physics, and I volunteered to teach her. She also invited her friend to join her, and I taught them both physics!

One evening, I was teaching them when the principal, who was an uncle of theirs, walked into the house. He spoke to Mohan's mother. I overheard him saying something about me. "What is that boy, Sinniah, doing here with these two girls in that room?"

"Oh, really sweet boy. He is teaching my daughter and her friend."

"Teaching? Teaching what?"

"Physics. He is supposed to be very good."

"What? Physics? He himself is a failure. What could he possibly be teaching here?"

That was the end of my teaching there.

We had a month to go before A levels—my second attempt. I was extremely nervous but not stressed. Sothy had a new haircut, and it was very impressive. "Where did you cut your hair, *machchan*?"

"Shaggy salon."

"Not Paramu or Muthu?" They were the two barbers who came to our hostels every month.

"No, not them. This is a new salon at the bus stand."

I went there. The salon was very colourful. The wall was painted blue. The floor was tiled with red ceramic tiles. The barber showed me some pictures of famous people, including a particular Hollywood actor. I had never seen his picture before.

The barber started to cut my hair as I fell asleep. When I woke up, I saw that he had placed a bowl on my head and was cutting all the hair that was outside the bowl. I was shocked to see that and protested. He told me that it was similar to the haircut of that famous actor whose picture he had showed me earlier. It was nothing like that. I had nothing to say and left after paying the bill. I wore a cap for the next two weeks and only removed it in the night after the lights were put out.

I went on to do my A levels again and this time got a B in applied mathematics and three passes (Ss).

The old lady woke me up.

"*Thamby*, we are nearing Fort. I hope you had a good sleep. You basically slept the entire time. I worry for you. I am old, and I will die in a few years' time. But you, *Thamby*, look after yourself. I wish you well."

"Sorry, Achchi. I told you a lot of lies. It was all in good spirit. I like you a lot, Achchi. Thanks for the rice parcel and barley. Take care, Achchi."

I took my brown box and suitcase. I moved down the corridor and stood next to the door. I kept looking outside. The railway track was moving fast. My dream had moved equally fast. I had dreamt of everything that my boarding life was.

I knew I had not done well. I knew I had wasted a lot of opportunities. I knew I'd let my parents down. I knew I'd let myself down. *What am I going to do? What will my dad say when he sees me? What's is in store for me?* We passed Maradana station, but the train didn't stop there. I was in the second carriage behind the engine. It was a long train.

The train was pulling into Fort. Tears were rolling down my cheeks. I was confused. I was down and out. I looked at Achchi. She smiled. She just had a small bag.

I saw Dadda and Ranjit Anna at the platform. My carriage moved past them. I was not sure if they saw me. I cried so much that Achchi offered me her handkerchief. "I am scared, Achchi. I am scared."

"*Thamby*, trust yourself. There must be something in you. Believe in yourself."

She got down first. I stood back. She took a few steps forward, turned, and looked into my eyes. She smiled again. "Believe… believe…believe," she mumbled.

She was gone.

I didn't want to get down. I stood still and let everyone out. I took those first steps down with fear and anxiety, not knowing where the next steps would take me.

THE REAL SURPRISE OF JULY '79

I SAW MUMMY STANDING IN FRONT OF ME, YELLING AT ME TO GET UP. I think it must have been around seven in the morning. It was another day, and surely another day of hope and disappointment.

I always wake up around seven and tune into the SLBC Tamil Service first thing after opening my eyes. The usual programme was their daily birthday greetings. I had no clue about the people being greeted but got a good kick out of listening to various people advertise their birthdays. After a quick shower, I'd take Ruki to school, come back home, and go straight back to bed.

I had no jobs, and I had no girlfriends. Life went on after I left St. John's. I spent my days looking at the rejection letters to my job applications, while in the evenings I would look in the *Daily News* employment section and apply for anything and everything.

Today, on this day, it was slightly different. I had to sit for a written test at the Chamber of Commerce. I had no idea what this was about. I had never even heard of Citibank.

Kitcha, my friend, came over to my house in the morning, as he too was going for the same interview. There was a massive intelligence gap between the two of us—it tipped negatively towards me. We started memorizing the capitals of all the countries. The last written test I had done was for a clerk's job at a bank, and that was a complete disaster. The questions were all about the capitals, English idioms, and names of organizations (like UNESCO).

This time, I had planned to prepare well, as I had already been to seventeen interviews. I had even auditioned for a role in a movie because I thought that I could impress them with my talking, but given my looks, I didn't think that would happen in a million years!

I was a bit irritated that I had to do all this studying for the written examination. For memorizing all the capital cities, we went in alphabetical order but went only up to *E*. I learnt that Addis Ababa is the capital of Ethiopia. Kitcha left for home to get ready for the interview, and I went back to bed.

I had a very formal interview routine. I would have a shower facing the window because someone had once told me that it brings good luck. I then OCed my brother's blue St. Michael's shirt and matched that with my best brown trousers. Ranjit Anna had a huge blue-and-yellow-checked tie that started at the left armpit and ended up at the right.

I continued to wear the Binco shoes. They were very shiny and hence very impressive. Just what was needed to complete the look. One didn't look under the soles, which trapped many small stones. I didn't eat anything that would upset my stomach. I have the most sensitive stomach in the world. Over the years, *koththu roti* and plain tea had destroyed it.

I walked down Park Road towards Havelock Road. I paused when I passed by the famous actress Geetha Kumarasinghe's house. The stones kept collecting in my shoes and were causing me some pain.

I waited for Bus Number 112 for about fifteen minutes, by which time about ten 112s had gone past in the opposite direction. Finally, I got onto the bus, and then came the most difficult part: buying the bus ticket—because I couldn't speak a word of Sinhalese. I asked the conductor for a ticket to Fort. He said something, and I gave him twenty cents. He said something else, and I gave him another twenty cents. He then shouted something else, for which I gave him another twenty cents. He then gave me the ticket with a balance of ten cents. I now knew it cost fifty cents to go to Fort. You learn something new every day!

There were so many people at the Chamber of Commerce, and they were all dressed very smartly. No one could match my tie, though. I met a lot of my old schoolmates. We talked about the examination paper. Most of my friends had been extremely good students at college. I, too, was good, but not at studies.

Kitcha told me that Citibank had advertised in *Time* magazine. I didn't know that such a magazine even existed. *Time* magazine? Was that a magazine about wristwatches? I knew the capitals up to Ethiopia. Would this be good enough? Someone else asked me whether I knew what OPEC was—"Oil-Producing European Countries"? Wrong! He quickly left me and moved on. My trump card was Ethiopia. I was waiting to show that off.

There were probably three hundred people in the examination hall. And there was another batch before us. My chances looked really slim, but I had to be optimistic. The hall was freezing. My blue St. Michael's shirt was not thick enough to keep this chill off.

There was a big guy standing in front of the hall. They said his name was Rifky Mackeen. I asked the guy next to me whether Rifky was the general manager. He replied confidently that Mr. Mackeen must be from Scotland. I immediately asked him the capital city of Scotland but was told that Scotland was not a separate country but part of the United Kingdom. I was sure that he hadn't studied up to *S*. I asked him what the capital of Ethiopia was, and he answered correctly.

The Scottish guy was very kind. He gave us hints about the paper and told us to take our time. The question paper contained three parts. Part one had two sets of numbers and two sets of words. They were to be matched. Part two was on arithmetic—we had to complete ninety sums in fifteen minutes. We were told that we would lose a mark for every wrong answer. This put a lot of pressure on me. The third part was to write an essay, and there were three topics. No capitals, no OPEC, no idioms. I picked the easiest topic and wrote about my school life. I didn't have much to say but hoped that whoever read my essay would feel sorry for me and do something about my being unemployed.

I had to put this examination behind me and get on with my life or lack thereof. I was giving maths tuition to three students who were studying for the O levels. That gave me sixty rupees every month, and I got another fifty rupees from my father. This was enough for me to go to the movies—I was watching six movies per week and still had money to go for rugby matches and buy two Tamil movie magazines.

I went for six more interviews, and they were all disastrous. I knew my capital cities for countries up to *E* and was good at sleeping. That hardly made me the choice candidate. I used to post three to four application letters a day. I was very desperate.

And then I gave up. My father was annoyed and told me that I should become a shepherd. My mum was, of course, helping me apply for jobs, and I knew that she sent some applications even without me knowing.

One day, I went to Kalpana Theatre for a movie. It was a very sad movie. There were three deaths, two suicides, and three murders. When I reached home, I was told that Citi had chosen me for a second interview at Turquand and Young's offices.

It suddenly crossed my mind that I should have learnt the capital cities for the second interview and not for the first. I then memorized all the capital cities and went through the same routine again. I showered facing the window and put on the same clothes and tie.

There were twelve people seated around a table. The Scottish guy, Mr. Mackeen, was seated to the far right of me. The panel asked me a lot of questions but nothing on capitals or about my hobbies. I had started collecting stamps the day before and had three stamps. I had to start a hobby, because that question about my hobbies came up in every interview. These formed part of the questions about my school life. I didn't have much to be proud of and thought that this was going to be another of those interviews.

They asked me if I had heard of Citibank, and I said that I had seen some advertisement in *Time* magazine. They said that almost everyone had said that. I wondered whether Kitcha had been there before me. I was glad that they didn't ask any more about it, because I had never seen or read a *Time* magazine.

I went back home and told my parents that I was not confident, and they were not surprised at all. That had been the story so far, so why would it change?

We didn't have a telephone in our house. My aunt, Baby Marmie, had one. I gave that telephone number—31982—so that I could be contacted whenever I went for interviews. Three days after the second oral interview, the phone rang.

I was asked to attend another interview in two days' time. This time, I felt good about it. When I went to TY's, I was ushered into a huge room. There were twelve of us there—Rajan, Vincent, Shyam, Lucky, Yvonne, Sabina, Fazeela, Chintha, the Scottish guy, Chong Quan, K. G. Bhat, and me.

Chong Quan opened the meeting and told us that we had all been selected. I almost wet my best brown trousers. I was so happy that I was trembling. He asked us all to introduce ourselves, and we did the rounds. The only thing I remember was that when Rajan introduced himself, saying that he was from the famous Royal College, Fazeela burst out, "M-P-H-O-T!" Everybody laughed, and I joined in. I had no idea what that meant or why everyone was laughing. It reminded me of the English movies that I went to where every time the people seated in the balcony laughed, we at the gallery joined in.

It was a fantastic feeling. I came to know that Mr. Mackeen was a Sri Lankan and that he too was joining us. This was the first group, and we started on the fifteenth of August 1979.

I would never in my life forget that fateful day, that beautiful afternoon. It was the beginning of a long affair with Citibank.

I was elated. At last I had achieved something, and I wanted to get to Park Road to share this piece of wonderful news with my family. I knew that I would now be accepted.

My only regret was that I hadn't had the opportunity to tell anyone that I knew the capital city of Ethiopia.

THIRTY-FIVE YEARS ON

"HELLO, HELLO…HELLO, HELLO?"

I was driving with my wife Anita next to me, and all my kids at the back. "Someone is trying to get me. Check the caller ID on the car phone, Anita."

"We can hear, Sinna. Seriously, why do you need to know now? Why can't you wait for another five minutes, and we will reach home." Anita was irritated.

"No, just check. What is your problem?"

"Dad, you can't be without being on the phone. It is only five minutes away," my kids chimed in.

Just one call had created an all-out war.

"Okay, don't worry." I was still keen to know who had called me. Then I heard two beeps, and I knew I got a text message, too.

"Ha, ha. Now what are you going to do? You want to know who is texting. Just concentrate on your driving and relax. You don't relax enough. Always restless."

They were all annoyingly right.

We came to a set of traffic lights close to my home at Walton-on-Thames. We had to stop for the red lights, and I quickly looked at the text. It was from my very good friend Gnanaponrajah. He and I had been classmates, hostel mates, and from Johnstone House. Whenever he called, I would immediately answer or call him back. He was now the principal of St. John's College. "Please call when free. Thanks," the text said.

I did call immediately from the car, with a lot of grumbling from Anita and kids, who were asked to remain quiet. "Hello. Sinniah here. You called?"

"Yes, Sinniah. About the prize-giving next year."

"What is it? What do you need?"

"No, Sinniah, can you be our chief guest?"

"What, me?"

"Yes, you and Anita. We need to discuss the dates."

"I am driving now, and I will call back."

That was a dream call. To have studied there from a young age and to be asked to go back as their chief guest was the utmost honour. "My school wants me as their chief guest," I proudly said to my family. "My school wants me…"

"Yes, Dad, we got it."

"Do you know the importance of this? Do you know how thrilled I am? This is my school, and they want me to return as their chief guest. I must prepare the speech."

"Sinna, it is one year ahead. Just drive carefully. Please, just worry about your driving."

"Anita, this is not a joke. My school—St. John's, Anita, St. John's—wants me as their chief guest. Oh my God!"

We reached home, and I called Sir, as I refer to him now. We set the date for 21 June 2014. I thanked him and said that it would be a great honour to be there. I told Anita to block that week off in the calendar at home.

I went into the bathroom and held my head in my hands and cried. I cried and cried for a long time.

I thought of my teachers, principals, cooks, and ground staff. I thought of them all. I knew that they would be shocked to hear that I was going to be their chief guest. I knew that they would be proud of me. They loved me even though I was a pain to all of them. They guided me in every possible way, and I was always grateful to all of them.

I continued to cry and I thought of that girl in the choir, I thought of the blue-dress girl at the convent, I thought of the beautiful nun, and I thought of my dear Sujatha, who had died a few years back.

I thought of my parents, my brothers, our family, my dear kids, and Anita. I felt proud and yet so humbled by it all.

Last, I thought of all my friends and my fellow boarders. Without them, I would never have made it through school. They tolerated me and were always there for me. "This is for them, this is for every one of them, this is for them," I kept on saying.

I stopped crying, and I wanted to really make this count. I wanted to make sure that I left the college boys with something meaningful. I wanted to tell them to look forward to a life of hope and happiness. This would be my gift to St. John's as it had gifted me.

Then I remembered the old lady, Achchi. How could I forget what she told me? "Believe…believe…believe."

I had decided that belief was what I would speak on.

We went to St. John's as chief guests and walked proudly down the aisle and up to the stage. After the English oratory was delivered, it was my turn to speak.

I thought of my parents and how much they had sacrificed for us to put us through this great school. My mother and my mother-in-law were in the first row. Dadda was not with us anymore, but he would have been proud of me.

I walked confidently to the podium. I felt overwhelmed but hid my emotions.

"Yes, Achchi. Let me do it."

And so I lifted my head and spoke:

The Honourable Chairman; Principal Sir; distinguished guests, staff, and students of St. John's; ladies and gentlemen:

Thank you very much for inviting my wife, Anita, and me here today as your guests of honour. It is indeed an honour, and I am deeply humbled to stand in front of you all.

St. John's College has a very long history, having been founded some one hundred ninety-one years ago. The education of life that this great institution provides is never evident when you are a student. It becomes evident only when you go out into the real world, where one is challenged. St. John's quietly enables us to face them all, to overcome and go forward. We sing, "Johnians always play the game." This doesn't just refer to sports, but it refers to the wider game of life.

Having spent almost all my school days at St. John's, I am eternally grateful for what I learnt here. The learning was endless and at times painful. The first few years of hostel life were tough. Forming friendships was challenging, as we came from so many different backgrounds. Sometimes it was difficult to get used to teachers who were such strict disciplinarians. But underneath all this, there was something special about St. John's that I can be very proud of. Today, the first thing I proudly say to anyone is, "I studied at St. John's College, Jaffna, Sri Lanka—the best school in the world!"

The innocent friendships that we formed some thirty-five years ago have grown from strength to strength. The fear we had for our teachers has turned into utmost respect and total loyalty. Most of all, our affection for St. John's continues to grow in every possible way.

I am not sure how many years have gone by since the first college prize-giving was held, but surely I must be the only chief guest who has never won a prize. Among this audience, I can see some very familiar faces. I see some of my former teachers who would never have dreamt that I would be standing here one day as the chief guest. I would like to say that it feels like a dream for me, too.

I want to begin by congratulating each and every one of you who has won a prize. This is a reflection of your hard work and dedication throughout the past year. Whether you won a prize for academic achievement, for achievements in sport, or in any other field, it is truly great to have your efforts richly rewarded and recognized. I am sure you made yourselves, your parents and family members, and all your teachers very proud. Well done, and I wish you all continued success.

When I was a student, we, the nonprizewinners, were always asked to sit at the back of the hall. As the winners were getting their well-deserved prizes, the one thing that constantly crossed my mind was, "Can I ever be successful?"

Today I want to speak to all of you—those who won prizes and those who, like me, are wondering whether they can ever be successful. I would like to tell you this: it is all up to you. It is you and you alone who can define your success. I want to really challenge you by asking a simple question: "Do you know how good you are to be successful?"

I want to tell you a story—a true story, where I was present. It happened on 24 April 2007 at Sabina Park, Kingston, Jamaica. It was a very hot and humid day when Sri Lanka took on New Zealand in the World Cup semifinals. It is the stand-out innings of Mahela Jayawardena that I would like to share with you.

The scorecard will tell us that Mahela scored one hundred and fifteen runs in one hundred and nine balls. But the scorecard will not tell you the hard work that went into getting there—how his innings was formed, how he was patient, how he let go of so many opportunities to score, and how he built partnerships. The scorecard will also not tell you how he used his strengths, and used them perfectly, to overcome the challenges he faced to build and deliver a great innings.

Most importantly, Mahela Jayawardena, the Sri Lankan captain, believed in himself. He knew he was good enough to deliver a quality innings. That was the key component of his success and of his beautiful innings that day.

Well, we all can learn a lot from that. We define our success by what is on the board or by the prizes we win. What success was for Tharanga that day was different to what it was for Mahela. Tharanga was judged by the explosive start that he gave to the innings, while Mahela was judged for the calm and steady way he settled for a long innings, accelerating at the end. Both of them were successful. It is therefore important to understand that all of us can and will achieve success through different routes.

It is my fundamental belief that every one of us has the capacity and capability to achieve success. It does not mean that we become overconfident and arrogant about our talents. It is about believing that we can!

When Mahela came to the crease, Tharanga was in full flow. The run rate was still around five, but Sri Lanka's batting was vulnerable, which even the opposing captain, Stephen Fleming, acknowledged at the toss.

Mahela knew that he, too, could join Tharanga and start scoring fast. He could have done that, but he didn't. He buckled down and scored very slowly, giving Tharanga the opportunity to score freely. He played carefully so that he could easily pick up his run rate later. That was his strength, and he was aware of that.

On the other hand, when I got through my ordinary-level examination with much difficulty, I believed that I should try to become a doctor. As you know, this was a prestigious profession—it was then, and I am sure it is now! I enrolled myself in the Bio stream despite the fact that I had failed biology. My first class was zoology, where I was given a frog to dissect and then had to draw it. When I finished drawing, my zoology teacher told me that my frog looked like a goat. Next day, I spoke to the principal and quickly transferred myself out of the Bio stream into Mathematics stream. I knew my limitations but tried to ignore them.

Successful people know and acknowledge their limitations. Your limitations will throw you challenges and obstacles. There is no point fighting them. It is better to overcome them; otherwise, they will hold you back from achieving success.

At the end of fortieth over, Sri Lanka had slowly built their innings to one hundred and eighty runs for the loss of four wickets. Mahela was not out at forty runs from seventy-four balls. The commentators were giving him a hard time. They were accusing him of taking too much time, saying that Sri Lanka had had a decent platform, and now they'd messed it up.

This is what happens in real life, too. People will judge us by what they expect from us without realizing that all of us have different paths to achieve success. The world will not know our limitations, the world will not know our strengths, and the world will not know the challenges we face. But the world will be quick to judge us according to what they expect from us.

That is where your own determination and drive will have to come in. That is how Mahela built his innings—he got to his fifty in the forty-first over and in seventy-six balls. What happened from there on was a privilege to watch—a brutal attack on the New Zealand bowling. He raced to one hundred in one hundred and four balls. The last fifty came up in twenty-eight balls and took Sri Lanka to two hundred and eighty-nine for the loss of five wickets. This was way over what was predicted. It was done solely by his sheer belief and careful execution.

As we go on to live our lives outside the school environment, we will have wickets falling around us. We will have commentators predicting what we can achieve and commend or condemn the way we bat. The challenge for us is not to allow these external factors to affect us. Do we allow these external pressures to stress us, or do we build our innings carefully and according to what we want to achieve and play a Mahela innings? To achieve success and bring the best out of you, you will need to withstand these external pressures and build your own innings.

One has to look back at Mahela's innings and admire the way he built it. He took a long time to lay a good foundation. His was a slow and steady innings. Likewise, success doesn't come overnight. One has to work for it patiently and build it up slowly. We should run a marathon, not a sprint. You will need to take your own time, according to your own plan and ability, and then go and achieve your own success!

When I was seated at that grounds, watching that match, and was getting frustrated by his innings, I never realized how well he was planning it. Cricinfo, the cricket website, described it as "an innings that has been worth its weight in gold." Every time the run rate was dropping, he would slowly squeeze in a four, and every time a wicket fell, he took on a slightly attacking role and then went back to playing a steady innings. He was reacting to the situation rather than worrying about it.

This is an incredible attribute that we all need. Every time we face a crisis or a challenge, we really need to take a step back, analyse the situation, and react—react positively. As they say, "the reaction to a challenge is more important than the challenge itself." There is no point in worrying about a wicket that falls, but it is important to figure out what needs to be done next. There is no point in worrying about not winning a prize, but you should think forward as to how to do better and thereby give yourself a chance to win a prize.

There are so many stories like Mahela's innings from which we can learn about life. Whether you are a prizewinner today or not, there are bigger and better things to look forward to in the future.

You will and you can achieve success:
By understanding your strengths and limitations.
By reacting positively to your challenges.
By accepting that your path could be different to that of others.
By being patient and building your life over a period of time.
And, most important:
By believing in yourself!

Before I finish, once again, I'd like to thank you all for inviting Anita and me. As I said at the outset, we are deeply touched and humbled to be here.

In closing, I would like to say to all of you again—believe in yourself! You have so much inside you that will make you very successful! Next time, don't ask yourself the question that I asked myself. Assure yourself by saying, "Yes, I can be successful."

And as the great boxer Muhammad Ali once said, "If my mind can conceive it and my heart can believe it, then I can achieve it."

Thank you very much.

ABOUT THE AUTHOR

BERNARD SINNIAH lives with his wife, Anita, and three kids at Walton-on-Thames, Surrey, United Kingdom.

Part of the sales proceeds of this book will be donated to Serendib Charitable Trust, a charity that is helping to rebuild Nuffield School for the Deaf and Blind at Kaithaddy, Jaffna, Sri Lanka.

Printed in Great Britain
by Amazon.co.uk, Ltd.,
Marston Gate.